Richard Murphy
Collected Poems 1952-2000

Richard Murphy

Collected Poems
1952-2000

WAKE FOREST UNIVERSITY PRESS

Published in North America
by Wake Forest University Press.
Copyright © Richard Murphy
First U.S. Edition published 2001
All rights reserved.

For permission,
required to reprint or broadcast
more than several lines, write to:
Wake Forest University Press
Post Office Box 7333
Winston-Salem, NC 27109

Printed in the United States by Thomson-Shore
Text set in Quadraat type
Library of Congress Catalogue Card Number 00-100480
ISBN 0-916390- 97-7 (paperback)
ISBN 0-916390- 98-5 (clothbound)

For my sister Mary

and in memory of her husband

Gerald H. Cookson

CONTENTS

PART FIVE. Sri Lanka and Poems of 1985–1992

PART SIX. The Price of Stone, 1981–1984

I

Sailing to an Island

AND POEMS OF 1952–1962

The boom above my knees lifts, and the boat
Drops, and the surge departs, departs, my cheek
Kissed and rejected, kissed, as the gaff sways
A tangent, cuts the infinite sky to red
Maps, and the mast draws eight and eight across
Measureless blue, the boatmen sing or sleep.

We point all day for our chosen island,
Clare, with its crags purpled by legend:
There under castles the hot O'Malleys,
Daughters of Granuaile, the pirate queen
Who boarded a Turk with a blunderbuss,
Comb red hair and assemble cattle.
Across the shelved Atlantic groundswell
Plumbed by the sun's kingfisher rod,
We sail to locate in sea, earth, and stone
The myth of a shrewd and brutal swordswoman
Who piously endowed an abbey.
Seven hours we try against wind and tide,
Tack and return, making no headway.
The north wind sticks like a gag in our teeth.

Encased in a mirage, steam on the water,
Loosely we coast where hideous rocks jag,
An acropolis of cormorants, an extinct
Volcano where spiders spin, a purgatory
Guarded by hags and bristled with breakers.

The breeze as we plunge slowly stiffens:
There are hills of sea between us and land,
Between our hopes and the island harbour.
A child vomits. The boat veers and bucks.
There is no refuge on the gannet's cliff.
We are far, far out: the hull is rotten,
The spars are splitting, the rigging is frayed,
And our helmsman laughs uncautiously.

What of those who must earn their living
On the ribald face of a mad mistress?
We in holiday fashion know
This is the boat that belched its crew
Dead on the shingle in the Cleggan disaster.

Now she dips, and the sail hits the water.
She luffs to a squall; is struck; and shudders.
Someone is shouting. The boom, weak as scissors,
Has snapped. The boatman is praying.
Orders thunder and canvas cannonades.
She smothers in spray. We still have a mast;
The oar makes a boom. I am told to cut
Cords out of fishing-lines, fasten the jib.
Ropes lash my cheeks. Ease! Ease at last:
She swings to leeward, we can safely run.
Washed over rails our Clare Island dreams,
With storm behind us we straddle the wakeful
Waters that draw us headfast to Inishbofin.

The bows rock as she overtakes the surge.
We neither sleep nor sing nor talk,
But look to the land where the men are mowing.
What will the islanders think of our folly?

The whispering spontaneous reception committee
Nods and smokes by the calm jetty.
Am I jealous of these courteous fishermen
Who hand us ashore, for knowing the sea
Intimately, for respecting the storm
That took nine of their men on one bad night
And five from Rossadillisk in this very boat?
Their harbour is sheltered. They are slow to tell
The story again. There is local pride
In their home-built ships.
We are advised to return next day by the mail.

But tonight we stay, drinking with people
Happy in the monotony of boats,

4

Bringing the catch to the Cleggan market,
Cultivating fields, or retiring from America
With enough to soak till morning or old age.

The bench below my knees lifts, and the floor
Drops, and the words depart, depart, with faces
Blurred by the smoke. An old man grips my arm,
His shot eyes twitch, quietly dissatisfied.
He has lost his watch, an American gold
From Boston gas-works. He treats the company
To the secretive surge, the sea of his sadness.
I slip outside, fall among stones and nettles,
Crackling dry twigs on an elder tree,
While an accordion drones above the hill.

Later, I reach a room, where the moon stares
Through a cobwebbed window. The tide has ebbed,
Boats are careened in the harbour. Here is a bed.

A solitary invalid in a fuchsia garden
Where time's rain eroded the root since Eden,
He became for a tenebrous epoch the stone.

Here wisdom surrendered the don's gown
Choosing, for Cambridge, two deck chairs,
A kitchen table, undiluted sun.

He clipped with February shears the dead
Metaphysical foliage. Old, in fieldfares
Fantasies rebelled though annihilated.

He was haunted by gulls beyond omega shade,
His nerve tormented by terrified knots
In pin-feathered flesh. But all folly repeats

Is worth one snared robin his fingers untied.
He broke prisons, beginning with words,
And at last tamed, by talking, wild birds.

Through accident of place, now by belief
I follow his love which bird-handled thoughts
To grasp growth's terror or death's leaf.

He last on this savage promontory shored
His logical weapon. Genius stirred
A soaring intolerance to teach a blackbird.

So before alpha you may still hear sing
In the leaf-dark dusk some descended young
Who exalt the evening to a wordless song.

His wisdom widens: he becomes worlds
Where thoughts are wings. But at Rosroe hordes
Of village cats have massacred his birds.

AUCTION

When furniture is moved
From a dead-free home
Through lean, loved
Rooms alone I come,

To bid for damp etchings,
My grandaunt's chair,
Drawers where rings
Of ruby in water flare.

A sacked gardener
Shows me yew hedges
House high, where
The dead made marriages.

With what shall I buy
From time's auctioneers
This old property
Before it disappears?

I lean on a lighthouse rock
Where the seagowns flow,
A trawler slips from the dock
Sailing years ago.

Wine, tobacco, and seamen
Cloud the green air,
A head of snakes in the rain
Talks away desire.

A sailor kisses me
Tasting of mackerel,
I analyse misery
Till Mass bells peal.

I wait for clogs on the cobbles,
Dead feet at night,
Only a tempest blows
Darkness on sealight.

I've argued myself here
To the blue cliff-tops:
I'll drop through the sea-air
Till everything stops.

You have netted this night
From the sea a vase
Which once we carried
At the festivals
In Phaestos where
A young prince ruled
And a stone leopard
Crouched on the walls
Guarding those granaries
And the golden bulls.

Until one April hour's
Earthquake of defeat
By galleys that grooved
Our unwary waters,
When the oil of peace
Blazed in every cruse,
Home became for us
The weltering sea
And language a hiss
In the wood of oars.

Then through gorges on the run
Alone I crawled
To a scorpion plain
Dry with poppies
To bury the stolen
Treasure of cities,
And I passed those years
Dumb below pines
A slave to the pleasures
Of the land of quince.

By the nets of your grace
My heart was hauled
From the heavy mud,

And tonight we sailed
To this island garden
Flaming with asphodel,
Moonlight raking
The early corn,
While the spades rang
On our lost foundation.

I have learnt to restore
From dust each room
The earthquakes lowered
In that doomed spring,
To piece beyond the fire
The cypress court
With gryphons basking,
Wander in the snow
Of almonds before
Those petals were wasting.

You have taken this night
Years of grievance
From the silted heart
And broken the script
Into household language,
You have cut into me
That gypsum field
Happy with harvesters
Fluting the sky
With sheaves on their shoulders.

TO A CRETAN MONK
IN THANKS FOR A FLASK OF WINE

God bless you Dionysus
For your wedding gift of wine
Poured from a ten-year seal
With prayers to make children
Where anemones through grass
Light on a terraced hill.

In midnight robes of a monk
And Byzantine chiselled beard
You decant us this drink
Laughing as a goatherd
Whose bells beside a spring
Open iris in my head.

God bless you Dionysus
For hectares of your grape
Manned by the dead in cypress
Where the labourers mope
And asphodel throws words
Wild in a season of cherry.

Ageing at mountain monastery
With rifles in your cell
Near cedar wood and rosemary
In remembrance you still
Hunt the planes of an enemy
Across the Cretan sky.

God bless you Dionysus now
The bees forsake my head
Mining the open sheaths
Your nectar resurrected
Where water of melting snow
Moves through a valley of leaves.

She grew ninety years through sombre winter,
Rhododendron summer of midges and rain,
In a beechwood scarred by the auctioneer,

Till a March evening, the garden work done,
It seemed her long life had been completed,
No further growth, no gaiety could remain.

At a wedding breakfast bridesmaids planted
With trowel and gloves this imported fir.
How soon, measured by trees, the party ended.

Arbour and crinoline have gone under
The laurel, gazebos under the yews:
Wood for wood, we have little to compare.

We think no more of granite steps and pews,
Or an officer patched with a crude trepan
Who fought in Rangoon for these quiet acres.

Axes and saws now convert the evergreen
Imperial shadows into deal boards,
And let the sun enter our house again.

Quickly we'll spend the rings that she hoarded
In her gross girth. The evening is ours.
Those delicate girls who earthed her up are faded.

Except for daffodils, the ground is bare:
We two are left. They walked through pergolas
And planted well, so that we might do better.

THE WOMAN OF THE HOUSE

In memory of my grandmother Lucy Mary Ormsby
whose home was in the west of Ireland
1873–1958

On a patrician evening in Ireland
I was born in the guest-room: she delivered me.
May I deliver her from the cold hand
Where now she lies, with a brief elegy?

It was her house where we spent holidays,
With candles to bed, and ghostly stories:
In the lake of her heart we were islands
Where the wild asses galloped in the wind.

Her mind was a vague and log-warmed yarn
Spun between sleep and acts of kindliness:
She fed our feelings as dew feeds the grass
On April nights, and our mornings were green:

And those happy days, when in spite of rain
We'd motor west where the salmon-boats tossed,
She would sketch on the pier among the pots
Waves in a sunset, or the rising moon.

Indian meal porridge and brown soda bread,
Boiled eggs and buttermilk, honey from gorse,
Far more than we wanted she always offered
In a heart-surfeit: she ate little herself.

Mistress of mossy acres and unpaid rent,
She crossed the walls on foot to feed the sick:
Though frugal cousins frowned on all she spent
People had faith in her healing talent.

She bandaged the wounds that poverty caused
In the house that famine labourers built,
Gave her hands to cure impossible wrong
In a useless way, and was loved for it.

Hers were the fruits of a family tree:
A china clock, the Church's calendar,
Gardeners polite, governesses plenty,
And incomes waiting to be married for.

How the feckless fun would flicker her face
Reading our future by cards at the fire:
Rings and elopements, love-letters, old lace,
A signet of jokes to seal our desire.

"It was sad about Maud, poor Maud!" she'd sigh
To think of the friend she lured and teased
Till she married the butler. "Starved to death,
No service either by padre or priest."

Cholera raged in the Residency:
"They kept my uncle alive on port."
Which saved him to slaughter a few sepoys
And retire to Galway in search of sport.

The pistol that lost an ancestor's duel,
The hoof of the horse that carried him home
To be stretched on chairs in the drawing-room,
Hung by the Rangoon prints and the Crimean medal.

Lever and Lover, Somerville and Ross
Have fed the same worm as Blackstone and Gibbon,
The mildew has spotted *Clarissa's* spine
And soiled the *Despatches of Wellington.*

Beside her bed lay an old Bible that
Her Colonel Rector husband used to read,
And a new *Writers' and Artists' Year-book*
To bring a never-printed girlhood back.

The undeveloped thoughts died in her head,
But from her heart, through the people she loved
Images spread, and intuitions lived,
More than the mere sense of what she said.

At last, her warmth made ashes of the trees
Ancestors planted, and she was removed
To hospital to die there, certified.
Her house, but not her kindness, has found heirs.

Compulsory comforts penned her limping soul:
With all she uttered they smiled and agreed.
When she summoned the chauffeur, no one obeyed:
A hearse would come to take her at nightfall.

"Order the car for nine o'clock tonight!
I must get back, get back. They're expecting me.
I'll bring the spiced beef and the nuts and fruit.
Come home and I'll brew you lime-flower tea!

"The house in flames and nothing is insured!
Send for the doctor, let the horses go.
The dogs are barking again. Has the cow
Calved in the night? What is that great singed bird?

"I don't know who you are, but you've kind eyes.
My children are abroad and I'm alone.
They left me in this gaol. You all tell lies.
You're not my people. My people have gone."

Now she's spent everything: the golden waste
Is washed away, silent her heart's hammer.
The children overseas no longer need her,
They are like aftergrass to her harvest.

People she loved were those who worked the land
Whom the land satisfied more than wisdom:
They've gone, a tractor ploughs where horses strained,
Sometimes sheep occupy their roofless room.

Through our inheritance all things have come,
The form, the means, all by our family:
The good of being alive was given through them,
We ourselves limit that legacy.

The bards in their beds once beat out ballads
Under leaky thatch listening to sea birds,
But she in the long ascendancy of rain
Served biscuits on a tray with ginger wine.

Time can never relax like this again,
She in her phaeton looking for folklore,
He writing sermons in the library
Till lunch, then fishing all the afternoon.

On a wet winter evening in Ireland
I let go her hand, and we buried her
In the family earth beside her husband.
Only to think of her, now warms my mind.

DROIT DE SEIGNEUR

1820

In a grey rectory a clergyman was reading
Fortunate by firelight the *Connaught Journal*.
The shutters were closed, for famine was spreading
Among the people. The portrait of Cromwell,
One hand on the Bible, the other on a sword,
Had been stowed that evening under a haystack.
The air was crackling with the whips of rhetoric.

A groom was saddling his mare in the stable
While a redcoat stumbled down the loft ladder
Buttoning his tunic, followed by a girl
Who ran to the kitchen. The yard lantern
Yellowed the stirrups and the buckled leather
On the mare's girth as he combed her down.
The master was for hunting the Ribbonmen:

A secret band, swearing oaths by moonlight,
Refusing to pay tithes or rent to the landlord,
Who battered on lonely doors after midnight,
And wore round their sleeves a white riband.
He called it his duty to commit these rogues
To the jury of gentlemen at Galway Assizes.
Saving of property went with saving of souls.

So he galloped out with a few soldiers
On to the gravelled road under the lime-trees
With his father's pistol in a handsome holster.
They ambushed a wedding from the next parish.
All escaped except a young simpleton
In whose pocket they found a white bandage.
Twenty miles to Galway he was marched in chains.

In the pigeon park the heifers were grazing
Under the beech-trees. The soldiers had gone.
Behind the frown of the windows, browsing

On the price of cattle in the *Connaught Journal*,
The rector looked out on the frost and the sun.
The girl ran across the yard with a bucket.
"Tomorrow," he read, "the boy will be executed."

Where the Corrib river chops through the Claddagh
To sink in the tide-race its rattling chain
The boatwright's hammer chipped across the water

Ribbing this hooker, while a reckless gun
Shook the limestone quay-wall, after the Treaty
Had brought civil war to this fisherman's town.

That "tasty" carpenter from Connemara, Cloherty,
Helped by his daughter, had half planked the hull
In his eightieth year, when at work he died,

And she did the fastening, and caulked her well,
The last boat completed with old Galway lines.
Several seasons at the drift-nets she paid

In those boom years, working by night in channels
With trammel and spillet and an island crew,
Tea-stew on turf in the pipe-black forecastle,

Songs of disasters wailed on the quay
When the tilt of the water heaved the whole shore.
"She was lucky always the *Ave Maria*,"

With her brown sails, and her sleek skin of tar,
Her forest of oak ribs and larchwood planks,
Cut limestone ballast, costly fishing gear,

Fastest in the race to the gull-marked banks,
What harbour she hived in, there she was queen
And her crew could afford to stand strangers drinks,

Till the buyers failed in nineteen twenty-nine,
When the cheapest of fish could find no market,
Were dumped overboard, the price down to nothing;

Until to her leisure a fisher priest walked
By the hungry dockside, full of her name,
Who made a cash offer, and the owners took it.

Then like a girl given money and a home
With no work but pleasure for her man to perform
She changed into white sails, her hold made room

For hammocks and kettles, the touch and perfume
Of priestly hands. So now she's a yacht
With pitch-pine spars and Italian hemp ropes,

Smooth-running ash-blocks expensively bought
From chandlers in Dublin, two men get jobs
Copper-painting her keel and linseeding her throat,

While at weekends, nephews and nieces in mobs
Go sailing on picnics to the hermit islands,
Come home flushed with health having hooked a few dabs.

⋆　⋆　⋆

Munich, submarines, and the war's demands
Of workers to feed invaded that party
Like fumes of the diesel the dope of her sails,

When the Canon went east into limed sheep-lands
From the stone and reed patches of lobstermen
Having sold her to Michael Schofield PC,

Who was best of the boatsmen from Inishbofin,
She his best buy. He shortened the mast, installed
A new "Ailsa Craig," made a hold of her cabin,

Poured over the deck thick tar slightly boiled;
Every fortnight he drained the sump in the bilge
"To preserve the timbers." All she could do, fulfilled.

The sea, good to gamblers, let him indulge
His fear when she rose winding her green shawl
And his pride when she lay calm under his pillage:

And he never married, was this hooker's lover,
Always ill-at-ease in houses or on hills,
Waiting for weather, or mending broken trawls:

Bothered by women no more than by the moon,
Not concerned with money beyond the bare need,
In this boat's bows he sheathed his life's harpoon.

A neap-tide of work, then a spring of liquor
Were the tides that alternately pulled his soul,
Now on a pitching deck with nets to hand-haul,

Then passing Sunday propped against a barrel
Winding among words like a sly helmsman
Till stories gathered around him in a shoal.

She was Latin blessed, holy water shaken
From a small whiskey bottle by a surpliced priest,
Madonnas wafered on every bulkhead,

Oil-grimed by the diesel, and her luck lasted
Those twenty-one years of skill buoyed by prayers,
Strength forged by dread from his drowned ancestors.

She made him money and again he lost it
In the fisherman's fiction of turning farmer:
The cost of timber and engine spares increased,

Till a phantom hurt him, ribs on a shore,
A hulk each tide rattles that will never fish,
Sunk back in the sand, a story finished.

                    ⋆   ⋆   ⋆

We met here last summer, nineteen fifty-nine,
Far from the missiles, the moon-shots, the money,
And we drank looking out on the island quay,

When his crew were in London drilling a motorway.
Pricing the priceless, I made a fair offer
For the *Ave Maria*, and he agreed to sell.

Then he was alone, stunned like a widower—
Relics and rowlocks pronging from the wall,
A pot of boiling garments, winter everywhere,

Especially in his bones, watching things fall,
Hooks of three-mile spillets, trammels at the foot
Of the unused double-bed—his mind threaded with all

The marline of his days twined within that boat,
His muscles' own shackles then staying the storm
Which now snap to bits like frayed thread.

*   *   *

So I chose to renew her, to rebuild, to prolong
For a while the spliced yards of yesterday.
Carpenters were enrolled, the ballast and the dung

Of cattle he'd carried lifted from the hold,
The engine removed, and the stale bilge scoured.
De Valera's daughter hoisted the Irish flag

At her freshly adzed mast this Shrove Tuesday,
Stepped while afloat between the tackle of the *Topaz*
And the *St. John*, by Bofin's best boatsmen,

All old as himself. Her ghostly sailmaker,
Her inherited boatwright, her dream-tacking steersman
Picked up the tools of their interrupted work,

And in memory's hands this hooker was restored.
Old men my instructors, and with all new gear
May I handle her well down tomorrow's sea-road.

DROWNING OF A NOVICE

At Easter he came
    with a March wind blowing,
A lapsed Benedictine
    whose mind was fabling

An island where the monks
    like cormorants
Fished from the rocks
    in black garments.

He thought he could quietly
    with his own boat
Be fed by the sea;
    and with a spade

In winter find cockles
    and clams to eat.
But for her novice
    the sea grew white

Flowers in her garden
    petalled with spray.
He had brought no chart
    and he lost his way.

Where was the pebbled cove
    and the famine cottage?
His piano playing fingers
    ached at the oars.

Book-disputes that he dreaded
    reared up in waves,
His catechized head
    was coldly doused.

Now his feet were washed
    in the sluicing bilges.
For his last swim
    there were no prizes.

When his dinghy went down
    at a sheer shore
And the swell slogging,
    his arms opened

As if to his mother,
    and he drowned.
An island beachcomber
    picked up an oar.

At evening time
From cocks of hay
Children come
To a green marquee
Pitched at the dock
Where trawlers lie,
To hear the clack
Of a dancer's shoes
And watch the trick
Of a conjuror's nose.

She sang as a child
With Marie Lloyd,
Ran wild
On the caravan road.
Now she is old
Her silks are soiled
There are holes in her shoes
And she feels a fake
While every night
She marries the duke.

She does not play
Her life story,
She tries to tease
With a tinsel fan,
An opera hat
And a silver cane—
"I'm Burlington Bertie
I rise at ten-thirty"—
While the summer rain
Seeps through the tent.

In a caravan fire
Her children were burnt.
Now all the lighter

Her merriment
On the creaking stage
To hide her rage.
Dance and deceive,
O dance and live!
While the haymakers sleep
She drouses on dope.

On a wet night, laden with books for luggage,
And stumbling under the burden of himself,
He reached the pier, looking for a refuge.

Darkly he crossed to the island six miles off:
The engine pulsed, the sails invented rhythm,
While the sea expanded and the rain drummed softly.

Safety on water, he rocked with a new theme:
And in the warmth of his mind's greenhouse bloomed
A poem nurtured like a chrysanthemum.

His forehead, a Prussian helmet, moody, domed,
Relaxed in the sun: a lyric was his lance.
To be loved by the people, he, a stranger, hummed

In the herring-store on Sunday crammed with drunks
Ballads of bawdry with a speakeasy stress.
Yet lonely they left him, "one of the Yanks."

The children understood. This was not madness.
How many orphans had he fathered in words
Robust and cunning, but never heartless.

He watched the harbour scouted by sea-birds:
His fate was like fish under poetry's beaks:
Words began weirdly to take off inwards.

Time that they calendar in seasons not in clocks,
In gardens dug over and houses roofed,
Was to him a see-saw of joys and shocks,

Where his body withered but his style improved.
A storm shot up, his glass cracked in a gale:
An abstract thunder of darkness deafened

The listeners he'd once given roses, now hail.
He'd burst the lyric barrier: logic ended.
Doctors were called, and he agreed to sail.

1960

CONNEMARA MARBLE

The cut is cooled by water
Douched where the discs revolve
To the drum of a far-off motor
Slicing the polished cliff,
While under the shapeless mountain
Marble masons ponder
Souvenirs in the chunks of stone.

That gritty green-gashed line!
Why whorl it with charm
Into ashtrays and shamrocks,
Round towers, Celtic crosses?
Old men who wind the crane
Seem careless of the harm
Done to the quarried stone.

The marble of mackerel wanes
In sun on a hooker's deck,
But in shops this marble shines
Or swings from a girl's neck:
Why do the makers falter
And carve a weaker shape
Than a fish iced on a slab?

THE CLEGGAN DISASTER

Off the west coast of Ireland in 1927

Five boats were shooting their nets in the bay
After dark. It was cold and late October.
The hulls hissed and rolled on the sea's black hearth
In the shadow of stacks close to the island.
Rain drenched the rowers, with no drying wind.
From strokes of the oars a green fire flaked
And briskly quenched. The shore-lights were markers
Easterly shining across the Blind Sound.

Five pieces of drift-net with a mesh of diamonds
Were paid from each stern. The webbed curtains hung
Straight from the cork-lines, and warps were hitched
To the strong stems, and the pine oars boarded.
The men in the boats drew their pipes and rested.

The tide fell slack, all the breakers were still.
Not a flicker of a fish, only the slow fall
Of the ocean there drawing out the last drops of sleep.
Soon they could feel the effort of the ebb
Yearning at the yarn, twitching their mooring-stones
Stealthily seawards. Two boats began to haul.

From the bows of a boat in the centre of the bay
Concannon watched and waited. On each far wing
He heard them hauling. He held in his hand
The strong hemp rope which stretched from the cork-line
So that his fingers could feel the cord throb
If the shoal struck the nets. But so far, nothing.

Why had those others hauled? They were old
And experienced boatsmen. One man on the quay
At Bofin warned him, "Sharpen your knife,
Be ready for trouble, cut away your nets.
Your crew is too young." Were they going home?

Would the night not remain calm enough to fill
The barrels in their barns with food for the winter?

He had respect for the sea. He gave away
A share of his catch at the Cleggan market.
No one who asked for a feed of fish was refused.
On Bofin island, he loafed on land,
Dozed through a hungry winter dreaming of boats,
And in summer wanted neither food nor sleep
While he gave his strength seriously to the sea.

He was sure of his boat, though small, well built.
Her ribs and her keel were adzed out of oak,
Her thole-pins were cut out of green holly,
And the grapnel was forged by the Cleggan smith.
Since the day she was launched, she had been lucky.

He was doubtful of his crew: three men and a boy
Who needed the money. Their land was poor,
But they had no heart for this work on water.
They helped each other. There were throngs of children
In thatched houses, whose lights they could see
Sparkling on the island, dim specks at Cleggan.
That night the best of boatsmen were on the bay
And many who wished they had waited by the fire.

In the dark before the moon rose, driftingly he smelt
Faintly on the water a floating oil
Bleeding from the nets where a blue-shark havocked
On the quivering tails of a mackerel shoal.
So he hauled until he reached the snarled threshes
Of the snapping shark, which he stunned across the rail
And clubbed with a foot-stick, bursting its blood.

Iron shouts clanged round the horseshoe bay
From the fetlock gap to the broad channel
As luck began to load the farthest nets,
And the green mackerel river raced through the water,

Crossed over the gunwales, and jetted fire
In the black braziers of the rolling bilges.

He thought, as the lucky stream continued to flow,
"There are three more pieces of net to be hauled.
If we're too greedy, we could sink the boat.
We have enough now to row home safely.
Cut them in time and return in the daylight.
Darker it's getting, with a north-west wind."

The night was like a shell, with long sea surges
Loudening from afar, though no one was listening.
Quickly they folded the nets and heaped the fish.
The moon was kindling. The sky smouldered like soot.
Warm gusts of air floated by, moist with dew.
Mackerel flapped in the bilges. A woman was calling,
Crying from the beach. A shiver rippled the spine
Of the stony headland. Then, on the glistening gong
Of the sleeping sea, terrible hailstones hammered.

A storm began to march, the shrill wind piping
And thunder exploding, as lightning flaked
In willow cascades, and bayonets of hail
Flashed over craters and hillocks of water.
All the boats were trapped. None had reached the pier.
The target of the gale was the mainland rocks.

The men began to pray. Stack-funnelled hail
Crackled in volleys, with blasts on the bows
Where Concannon stood to fend with his body
The slash of seas. Then sickness surged,
And against their will they were griped with terror.
He told them to bail. When they lost the bailer
They bailed with their boots. Then they cast overboard
Their costly nets and a thousand mackerel.

She was drifting down the sound, her mooring-stone lifted
By the fingers of the tide plucking at the nets
Which he held with scorching hands. Over and over

He heard in his heart, "Keep her stem to the storm,
And the nets will help her to ride the water;
Meet the force of the seas with her bows,
Each wave as it comes." He'd use the knife later.

Down in the deep where the storm could not go
The ebb-tide, massive and slow, was drawing
Windwards the ninety-six fathom of nets
With hundreds of mackerel thickly meshed,
Safely tugging the boat off the mainland shore.
The moon couldn't shine, the clouds shut her out,
But she came unseen to sway on his side
All the waters gathered from the great spring tide.

As he slid from the cliff-slope of a heaped wave
Down the white and violet skin of turbulence
Into the boiling trough, he gathered in
Loose hanks of net, until the scalding rope
Steamed from his hands, the brittle boat, convulsed
By the far crest, shot through the spindrift safe.

The oarsmen were calling Concannon to let go,
Take it easy for a while. Let the boat drift
To the Cleggan shore, down wind, till they touch land.
Even there, if they died, it would be in a bay
Fringed with friends' houses, instead of in the open
Ocean, where the lost would never be found,
Where nothing is buried, no prayers are said.
Concannon silenced them, and stiffened his hold.

Twice the lightning blinked, then a crash of thunder.
Three cliffs of water rose above them, waves
Broke in his face, he fell down, and was dazed.

The wind began to play, like country fiddlers
In a crowded room, with nailed boots stamping
On a stone cottage floor, raising white ashes.
The sea became a dance. He staggered to the floor
As the music unleashed him, spun in a circle.

Now he was dancing round the siege of Death:
Now he was Death, they were dancing around him,
White robed dancers with crowns and clubs,
With white masked faces, and hands like claws
Flaying his eyes, as they clinched and swung.
He was holding the rope as the dance subsided.

While he lay there stunned, he remembered the sea
In tar-melting sunlight, dry weed on the thwarts,
The gills of mackerel tight in the meshes,
Hot stench of dead fish in the bailer,
Planks gaping wide, and thole-pins screeching,
The lines like lathes grooving the gunwales
While the depths yielded up the sacred John Dory.
He would never say, like that cripple on the quay,
He wished he had not wasted his life on the sea.

He knelt against the stem, his hands bleeding,
His eyes, scalded by the scurf of salt,
Straining to give shape to the shadows they saw
That looked like men in the milder water.
One of the crew said he heard his brother
Shouting for help, two oars away,
Yet when he hollowed, there was no reply.
In a lightning flash, a white hand rose
And rested on the gunwale, then slowly sank.

Down the valleys of this lull, like a black cow
In search of her calf, an upturned hull
Wallowed towards them. Her stem had parted.
All hands must have been lost. She lunged to his side
And almost staved him. Were the men inside?
Those who had thrown him his ropes from the quay?
The one who had warned him about his crew?
No help for them now. With his foot on her planks
He fended her off. As she bore away,
Her keel like a scythe cut a clear white swath
Through the gale's acres. Then a great sea crossed.
On the far side, as he nipped among white horses

Bolting towards him, under the streamers of manes
And the quick hoof-lash, he still headed the storm:
The chargers' lances hurtled with little harm
Through the icy air, while their hooves plunged on.

Now, though sea-boils encrusted his eyes,
He saw the Lyon Light, in spurts when they rode
Upon grey shoulders, flicker from white to red.
Lumps of water licked across tidal shallows.
They cantered at walls, and then faced hills.
The horses stampeded, as lanes closed ahead
In a white chalk-cliff. Rolled under horses
With manes in their mouths, their bones smashed,
Their blood washed away . . . Yet the cliff was passing.
The water rose to the thwarts. They went on bailing.

What were those lights that seemed to blaze like red
Fires in the pits of waves, lifted and hurled
At the aching sockets of his eyes, coals that lit
And expired in the space of a swell's slow heave?
"Am I going blind? *Am I going blind?*" he thought.
"Look at that wave. How it sharpens into a rock.
WATCH THAT ROCK. GET READY TO JUMP. It's gone.
Now *there's* a light . . . count the seconds: a slow pulse.
I can see that light from my own back door,
Slyne Head, never so high, such piercing brightness.
Where has it gone? Was it south of us it shone?
Lucky the keepers are safe. What a lonely life.
Lamps on the headlands have all been snuffed
By smothering waves. What weak pulse in the stars.
If I knew how to read them, we were saved."

Lights flickered and vanished. Like a grey seal
Blinded by shot, he clung to the stem, his eyes closed.
The boy cried out: "There's rocks to leeward."
"What rocks do you think?" another asked.
"Dog Rock, I think, I fished here last summer."
Concannon opened his knife: "I'm cutting the nets."
Piece by piece he slashed, but he had to tear

The clinging hanks with his finger bones, at last
He severed the rope, their guide on that dire sea-road,
And sank to his knees. The boatsmen rowed,
Backwards, falling away, her stem still to the storm,
With their eyes fixed on the faint lamps
That led across calm waters to Cleggan Quay.

It was three o'clock when she nudged the steps.
Safe on the stone bollards they fastened their ropes.
The full moon was whitening the ribs of hulks
In the worm-dark dock. The tide was flowing
As they trudged to the village. His crew helped him:
The sea had not claimed him, she had left him blind.

Lanterns shafted from the gates of the fish-store
Freshly that night cleaned for a ceili.
Bodies of fishermen lay on the floor on boxes,
Blood on their faces. Five had been found
By troops of searchers on shingle and sand.
Over the bier, with one hand cupping a flame,
An old man was looking at his drowned son.

As the day dawned, gap after gap was filled.
One of the boats was found on the beach at Letter
And floated off on the morning tide.
Only one body was got, the skull fractured:
Above high-water mark he had crawled and died.
The walking-stick of a man who was lame
Was thrown in a heap of rods on a silver strand.
There was a king of the Mayo fishermen
Drawn from the sea in the chain of his own nets.
Of those who survived, a young one was seen
Walking at noon in the fields, clutching a bailer.

A sleep, cordoned by memories, calmed the sea.
Dead bracken was rusting the headlands,
The hills were flaked with hoarfrost, the sky marbled
Like mackerel netted in June water
When the men were returning home to the island.

Concannon felt his eyes like smithy troughs
Where hot harpoons are plunged, they boiled with pain.
Blindly he rowed, facing the hidden sun.

They passed the tower in the harbour's mouth
Snow-white on the gun rock, the two round towers
Touching each other on green fields, the castle
Of Cromwell's crimes full of screeching choughs.
Women in shawls on the quay were waiting.

The funeral boats brought over the bodies found,
But most were carried away on the great ebb tide.
From the village of Rossadillisk they lost sixteen
And from Bofin nine. One man above all was blind.

In a common grave that was dug in the sand dunes
Close to high water mark but leagues from low springs
They laid side by side the pinewood coffins
Lowering them on ropes, then shovelled the fine sand
Which whisperingly slid round their recent companions,
And sometimes the shovels met with a knelling clang
While in shifts they worked till the mound was raised.

After the prayers were said and the graveyard closed
Concannon was counting the fifty steps to his house,
Working out sounds, the sea-fall on the beach.
Would the islanders ever again dare to fish?
When he'd mastered this dark road, he himself would ask
To be oarsman in a boat, and mend the nets on land.
The croak of a herring gull tolled across the sky.
An oystercatcher squealed. Shoals broke on the bay.
The flood tide rose and covered the deserted strand.

(YEARS LATER)

Whose is that hulk on the shingle
The boatwright's son repairs
Though she has not been fishing
For thirty-four years
Since she rode the disaster?

The oars were turned into rafters
For a roof stripped by a gale.
Moss has grown on her keel.

Where are the red-haired women
Chattering along the piers
Who gutted millions of mackerel
And baited the spillet hooks
With mussels and lugworms?
All the hurtful hours
Thinking the boats were coming
They hold against those years.

Where are the barefoot children
With brown toes in the ashes
Who went to the well for water,
Picked winkles on the beach
And gathered sea-rods in winter?
The lime is green on the stone
Which they once kept white-washed.
In summer nettles return.

Where are the dances in houses
With porter and cakes in the room,
The reddled faces of fiddlers
Sawing out jigs and reels,
The flickering eyes of neighbours?
The thatch which was neatly bordered
By a fringe of sea-stones
Has now caved in.

Why does she stand at the curtains
Combing her seal-grey hair
And uttering bitter opinions
On land work and sea fear,
Drownings and famines?
When will her son say,
"Forget about the disaster,
We're mounting nets today!"

GROUNDS, 1959

You were not there. I don't know who
That morning lit your cigarette:
But I was there because of you
To take the consequence of deceit
Asking a man in a wig, who'd not
Known or loved you, to interfere
Between us and our daughter.

Four years ago a civil farce
Was paid for, and they dragged in God,
Contracts, champagne, telegrams, cars:
But now needless pomp had dwindled
To needless echoes — "Yes, m'Lud,"
"No, m'Lud" — and I had lost you,
Lost everything we had gone through.

In white letters on black paper
A judge decreed we were dissolved
From all the good we owed each other,
From all the bad left unresolved.
What we were hangs dead in the air
As dust from a second-hand book
Picked off a shelf and put back.

In a dream you appear to me — sick
And lost in rain on a high cliff
Crying and careless where you walk.
A lighthouse flashes far, far off:
But I cannot, though I try to, speak
To stop the harm in all I've done
Dragging you down and down.

Horny sheep were encroaching
On our marriage bed
And wild goats rampaging
In and out of my head,

As I woke in a mystery
To the slang of gulls
On a barren rock promontory
Humanised by animals.

Across the bay a waterfall
Laughed at the rising sun
As my homecoming salmon
Spawned in your otter pool.

Now I watch you walking
Perfectly alive
And hear you talking
In the heyday of our love,

As I prepare to die
Long after you are dead,
Remembering how hard and why
Those hooves trampled.

2

The Battle of Aughrim

1962–1967

The God Who Eats Corn

1963

The battle of Aughrim (literally *horse-ridge*) was fought on the evening of Sunday, July 12, 1691, about seventeen miles southwest of Athlone, almost in the centre of Ireland. It was a bloodier battle than the Boyne (1690), with four times as many casualties, and decisive in establishing Protestant rule over the whole of Ireland for the next two hundred years.

The Irish army was a native force, equipped by Louis XIV, and commanded by the French Marquis of St. Ruth. Paid in brass, it fought in the name of King James II, an exile at St. Germain, and in the Catholic interest.

The English army, aiding the planters in Ireland, was largely a force of foreigners, drawn from seven nations opposed to Louis, and commanded by a Dutch general, Baron Ginkel. Paid in silver and gold, it fought in the names of King William and Queen Mary (nephew and daughter of James), in the Protestant interest.

Since the previous summer, when James had been defeated by William at the Boyne, the Irish Jacobites continued to hold out in Connaught, led by the ageing viceroy, the Duke of Tyrconnel. Patrick Sarsfield, Governor of the western province, a major-general of the army, had saved the besieged town of Limerick by a daring raid on William's supplies in August. But though James had given Sarsfield the title Earl of Lucan, he had appointed a Frenchman Commander-in-Chief of the Irish army. St. Ruth arrived at Limerick in May, lost Athlone by vanity and carelessness in June, and decided to stand at Aughrim on July 12 to restore his position and redeem his name.

Patrick Sarsfield disputed this hazardous strategy: his policy was to avoid risking the remnant of his nation in one great combat. St. Ruth dismissed Sarsfield to the rear of the army, to command the reserve, and gave him no information about the battle. The Irish, strongly placed on the hill, held off the allied onslaught until St. Ruth's decapitation. Then a traitor, Colonel Henry Luttrell, withdrew his cavalry from a vital pass. Sarsfield could do no more than cover the retreat to Limerick, where he signed the Treaty, and in

October sailed to France with ten thousand troops (known as the Wild Geese) to join the Irish Brigade. Two years later, a *maréchal-de-camp*, he was mortally wounded at Landen in the French victory over William of Orange.

1. Now

ON BATTLE HILL

Who owns the land where musket-balls are buried
In blackthorn roots on the esker, the drained bogs
Where sheep browse, and credal war miscarried?
Names in the rival churches are written on plaques.

Behind the dog-rose ditch, defended with pikes,
A tractor sprays a rood of flowering potatoes:
Morning fog is lifting, and summer hikers
Bathe in a stream passed by cavalry traitors.

A Celtic cross by the road commemorates no battle
But someone killed in a car, Minister of Agriculture.
Dairy lorries on the fast trunk-route rattle:
A girl cycles along the lane to meet her lover.

Flies gyrate in their galaxy above my horse's head
As he ambles and shies close to the National School—
Bullets under glass, Patrick Sarsfield's *Would to God* . . .—
And jolts me bareback on the road for Battle Hill:

Where a farmer with a tinker woman hired to stoop
Is thinning turnips by hand, while giant earth-movers
Shovel and claw a highway over the rector's glebe:
Starlings worm the aftergrass, a barley crop silvers,

And a rook tied by the leg to scare flocks of birds
Croaks as I dismount at the death-cairn of St. Ruth:
Le jour est à nous, mes enfants, his last words:
A cannonball beheaded him, and sowed a myth.

GREEN MARTYRS

I dream of a headless man
Sitting on a charger, chiselled stone.

A woman is reading from an old lesson:
". . . who died in the famine.

"Royal bulls on my land,
I starved to feed the absentee with rent.

"Aughrim's great disaster
Made him two hundred years my penal master.

"Rapparees, whiteboys, volunteers, ribbonmen,
Where have they gone?

"Coerced into exile, scattered
Leaving a burnt gable and a field of ragwort."

July the Twelfth, she takes up tongs
To strike me for a crop of calf-bound wrongs.

Her weekly half-crowns have built
A grey cathedral on the old gaol wall.

She brings me from Knock shrine
John Kennedy's head on a china dish.

ORANGE MARCH

In bowler hats and Sunday suits,
Orange sashes, polished boots,
Atavistic trainbands come
To blow the fife and beat the drum.

Apprentices uplift their banner
True blue dyed with "No Surrender!"
Claiming Aughrim as if they'd won
Last year, not 1691.

On Belfast silk, Victoria gives
Bibles to kneeling Zulu chiefs.
Read the moral, note the date:
"The secret that made Britain great."

Derry, oakwood of bright angels,
Londonderry, dingy walls
Chalked at night with "Fuck the Queen!"
Bygone canon, bygone spleen.

CASEMENT'S FUNERAL

After the noose, and the black diary deeds
Gossiped, his fame roots in prison lime:
The hanged bones burn, a revolution seeds.
Now Casement's skeleton is flying home.

A gun salutes, the troops slow march, our new
Nation atones for her shawled motherland
Whose welcome gaoled him when a U-boat threw
This rebel quixote soaked on Banna Strand.

Soldiers in green guard the draped catafalque
With chalk remains of once ambiguous bone
Which fathered nothing till the traitor's dock
Hurt him to tower in legend like Wolfe Tone.

From gaol yard to the Liberator's tomb
Pillared in frost, they carry the freed ash,
Transmuted relic of a death cell flame
Which purged for martyrdom the diarist's flesh.

On the small screen I watch the packed cortège
Pace from High Mass. Rebels in silk hats now
Exploit the grave with an old comrade's speech:
White hair tossed, a black cape flecked with snow.

HISTORICAL SOCIETY

I drive to a symposium
    On Ireland's Jacobite war,
Our new élite in a barrack room
    Tasting vintage terror.

Once an imperial garrison
    Drank here to a king:
Today's toast is republican,
    We sing "A Soldier's Song."

One hands me a dinted musket ball
    Heated by his palm.
"I found this bullet at Aughrim
    Lodged in a skull."

SLATE

Slate I picked from a nettlebed
Had history, my neighbour said.

To quarry it, men had to row
Five miles, twelve centuries ago.

An inch thick, it hung watertight
Over monks' litany by candlelight:

Till stormed by viking raids, it slipped.
Four hundred years overlapped.

Pirates found it and roofed a fort
A mile west, commanding the port.

Red-clawed choughs perched on it saw
Guards throw priests to the sea's jaw.

Through centuries of penal gale
Hedge-scholars huddled where it fell.

Pegged above a sea-wormed rafter
It rattled over landlord's laughter.

Windy decades pined across
Barrack roof, rebellion, moss.

This week I paved my garden path
With slate St. Colman nailed on lath.

INHERITANCE

Left a Cromwellian demesne
My kinsman has bulldozed three bronze age raths.

No tree can survive his chainsaw:
Hewing is part of the land reclamation scheme.

He has auctioned grandfather's Gallipoli sword
And bought a milking machine.

Slate he stripped from a Church of Ireland steeple
Has broadened his pigsty roof:

Better a goat's hoof in the aisle
Than rosary beads or electric guitars.

Five hundred cars pass the stone lion gates
For a civil war veteran's funeral.

On a grave behind a petrol pump
The wind wraps a newspaper around an obelisk.

On ancient battleground neat painted signs
Announce "Gouldings Grows."

CHRISTENING

A side-car creaks on the gravel drive,
The quality arrive.

With Jordan water
They mean to give me a Christian start.

Harmonium pedals squeak and fart.
I'm three weeks old.

It's a garrison world:
The good are born into the Irish gentry.

What do they hope my use of life will be?
Duty.

Fight the good fight:
Though out of tune, if loud enough, it's right.

Under the Holy Table there's a horse's skull
Shot for a landlord's funeral:

From a religious duel
The horse cantered the wounded master home.

Two clergy christen me: I'm saved from Rome.
The deaf one has not heard my name,

He thinks I am a girl.
The other bellows: "It's a boy, you fool!"

HISTORY

One morning of arrested growth
An army list roll-called the sound
Of perished names, but I found no breath
In dog-eared inventories of death.

Touch unearths military history.
Sifting clay on a mound, I find
Bones and bullets fingering my mind:
The past is happening today.

The battle cause, a hand grenade
Lobbed in a playground, the king's viciousness
With slaves succumbing to his rod and kiss,
Has a beginning in my blood.

2. Before

The story I have to tell
Was told me by a teacher
Who read it in a poem
Written in a dying language.
Two hundred and fifty years ago
The poet recalled
Meeting a soldier who had heard
From veterans of the war
The story I have to tell.

Deep red bogs divided
Aughrim, the horse's ridge
Of garland hedgerows and the summer dance,
Ireland's defence
From the colonists' advance:
Twenty thousand soldiers on each side,
Between them a morass
Of godly bigotry and pride of race,
With a causeway two abreast could cross.

In opposite camps our ancestors
Ten marriages ago,
Caught in a feud of absent kings
Who used war like a basset table
Gambling to settle verbal things,
Decide if bread be God
Or God a parable,
Lit matches, foddered horses, thirsted, marched,
Halted, and marched to battle.

"Gentlemen and Fellow Souldiers," said the Marquis of St. Ruth, addressing the Irish army with a speech found on the body of his secretary, and quoted by the Reverend George Story in *An Impartial History of the Wars of Ireland*.

"I Suppose it is not unknown to you, and the whole Christian World, what Glory I have acquired, and how Successful and Fortunate I have been in Suppressing Heresie in France, and propagating the Holy Catholick Faith, and can without Vanity boast my Self the happy Instrument of bringing over thousands of poor deluded Souls from their Errours, who owe their Salvation to the pious care of my thrice Illustrious Master, and my own Industry, assisted by some holy Members of our unspotted Church: while great numbers of those incourigable Hereticks have perished both Soul and Body by their obstinacy.

"It was for this reason that the most Puissant King my Master, Compassionating the miseries of this Kingdom, hath chosen me before so many worthy Generals to come hither, not doubting but by my wonted Diligence I should Establish the Church in this Nation, on such a foundation as it should not be in the power of Hell or Hereticks hereafter to disturb it: And for the bringing about of this Great and Glorious Work, next the Assistance of Heaven, the unresistable Puisance of the King my Master, and my own Conduct; the great dependance of all good Catholicks is on your Courage.

"I must confess since my coming amongst you, things have not answered my wishes, but they are still in a posture to be retrieved, if you will not betray your Religion and Countrey, by an unseasonable Pusilanimity.

"I'm assured by my Spyes, that the Prince of Oranges Heretical Army, are resolved to give us Battle, and you see them even before you ready to perform it. It is now therefore, if ever that you must indeavour to recover your lost Honour, Priviledges and Fore-fathers Estates: You are not Mercinary Souldiers, you do not fight for your Pay, but for your Lives, your Wives, your Children, your Liberties, your Country, your Estates; and to restore the most Pious of Kings to his Throne: But above all for the propagation of the Holy Faith, and the subversion of Heresie. Stand to it therefore my Dears, and bear no longer the Reproaches of the Hereticks, who Brand you with Cowardise, and you may be assured that King James will Love and Reward you: Louis the Great will protect you; all good Catholicks will applaud you; I my self will Command you; the Church will pray for you, your Posterity will bless you; Saints and Angels will Caress you; God will make you all Saints, and his holy Mother will lay you in her Bosome."

MARTIAL LAW

A country woman and a country man
Come to a well with pitchers,
The well that has given them water since they were children:
And there they meet soldiers.

Suspecting they've come to poison the spring
The soldiers decide to deal
Justly:
So they hang them on a tree by the well.

THE SHEEPFOLD

On Kelly's land at Aughrim, all is the same
As the old people remember, and pray it will be,
Where his father grazed sheep, like all before him.

Mullen the herd, propped by a fallen tree,
His mouth scabbed and his cheeks pitted by pox,
Blows on a reed pipe a fatal melody.

Ripe seeds are bending the tall meadowstalks.
He stops, when the sun sparks on a cuirass,
A goatskin drum across the sheepwalk tucks.

★

Buff-coated horsemen jump the walls, and press
The bleating flock, while Kelly pleads for pay:
"By the Holy Virgin, give us gold, not brass!"

Raw lancers goad their footsore ewes away
With rancid udders drained by thriving lambs:
"Do you grudge men food who fight for you?" they say.

Soon they reach camp, where flies hover in swarms
On entrails at the bivouacs, and they smoke
The meat on spits, lice crawling in their uniforms.

★

Farmer and herd follow with crook and stick,
Their grey slack tweed coats tied with twists of straw,
Reeking of wool and sour milk and turf smoke,

Up hill through hedgegaps to an ancient rath
Embanked by hawthorn, where the Catholic flag
Blazoned with Bourbon lilies for St. Ruth

Floats white and gold above a deep red bog,
And here they halt, blessing themselves, and kneel:
"Christ make the Frenchman pay us for our flock!"

*

Inside, they see a hand with a swan quill
That writes and writes, while powdered clerks translate,
Quoting with foreign voice the general's will:

"Children, I bring from France no better aid
To toast the image-wreckers on hell fire
Than my own skill to lead your just crusade.

"It is your duty, since I wage this war
For your souls' sake, to lose your flock, but win
A victory for your conscience and my honour."

*

"Give back our fleeces!" begs the shepherd, then
St. Ruth's head rises: "*Foutez-moi le camp!*"
Guards dash steel halberds, and the natives run.

Through glacial esker, by the river Suck
They choose the bog path to the richer camp
With tongues to talk and secret prayers for luck.

All day packhorses laden westwards tramp
Trundling bronze cannon behind casques of shot,
While eastwards, armed with spite, two traitors limp.

*

The Danish mercenaries they chance to meet
Standing in hogweed, sheltered by a ditch,
Assume they're spies, with no one to translate,

So fetch them to a grey house, where the Dutch
Commander who serves England's Orange king
Shakes hands, and gives them each a purse to clutch,

While a blond adjutant runs off to bring
The gunner Trench, who'll need their eyes next day,
When the cold cannon mouths start uttering.

MERCENARY

"They pick us for our looks
To line up with matchlocks,
Face shot like sandbags,
Fall, and manure the grass
Where we wouldn't be let trespass
Alive, but to do their work
Till we dropped in muck.

"Who cares which foreign king
Governs, we'll still fork dung,
No one lets us grab soil:
Roman or English school
Insists it is God
Who must lighten our burden
Digging someone else's garden."

DRAGOON

"I share a tent with Dan, smelling of seals
Whose oil he smears on his French matchlock
Drooling idly for hours about camp girls.

Polishing his plug bayonet, he boasts he'll hack
From a shorn heretic a pair of testicles
To hang above St. Brigid's Well for luck.

Soft west wind carries our friary bells
Against the tide of psalms flooding the plain.
Now Dan fills a powderhorn, his cheek swells.

'Learn him our creed,' he says, 'garotte your man:
Tomorrow night we'll eat like generals.'
Our supper meat is prodded, sniffed by Dan."

GOD'S DILEMMA

God was eaten in secret places among the rocks
His mother stood in a cleft with roses at her feet
And the priests were whipped or hunted like stags.

God was spoken to at table with wine and bread
The soul needed no heavenly guide to intercede
And heretics were burnt at stakes for what they said.

God was fallen into ruins on the shores of lakes
Peasants went on milking cows or delving dikes
And landlords corresponded with landlords across bogs.

PLANTER

Seven candles in silver sticks,
Water on an oval table,
The painted warts of Cromwell
Framed in a sullen gold.
There was ice on the axe
When it hacked the king's head.
Moths drown in the dripping wax.

Slow sigh of the garden yews
Forty years planted.
May the God of battle
Give us this day our land
And the papists be trampled.
Softly my daughter plays
Sefauchi's Farewell.

Dark night with no moon to guard
Roads from the rapparees,
Food at a famine price,
Cattle raided, corn trod,
And the servants against us
With our own guns and swords.
Stress a hymn to peace.

Quiet music and claret cups,
Forty acres of green crops
Keep far from battle
My guest, with a thousand troops
Following his clan-call,
Red-mouthed O'Donnell.
I bought him: the traitor sleeps.

To whom will the land belong
This time tomorrow night?

I am loyal to fields I have sown
And the king reason elected:
Not to a wine-blotted birth mark
Of prophecy, but hard work
Deepening the soil for seed.

RAPPAREES

Out of the earth, out of the air, out of the water
And slinking nearer the fire, in groups they gather:
Once he looked like a bird, but now a beggar.

This fish rainbows out of a pool: "Give me bread!"
He fins along the lake shore with the starved.
Green eyes glow in the night from clumps of weed.

The water is still. A rock or the nose of an otter
Jars the surface. Whistle of rushes or bird?
It steers to the bank, it lands as a pikeman armed.

With flint and bundles of straw a limestone hall
Is gutted, a noble family charred in its sleep,
And they gloat by moonlight on a mound of rubble.

The highway trees are gibbets where seventeen rot
Who were caught last week in a cattle raid.
The beasts are lowing. "Listen!" "Stifle the guard!"

In a pinewood thickness an earthed-over charcoal fire
Forges them guns. They melt lead stripped from a steeple
For ball. At the drumming of a snipe each can disappear

Terrified as a bird trapped in a gorse fire,
To delve like a mole or mingle like a nightjar
Into the earth, into the air, into the water.

3. During

St. Ruth trots on a silver mare
Along the summit of the ridge,
Backed by a red cavalcade
Of the King's Life Guards.
He wears a blue silk tunic,
A white lace cravat,
Grey feathers in his hat.

He has made up his mind to put
The kingdom upon a fair combat:
Knowing he cannot justify
Losing Athlone
Before his Most Christian master,
He means to bury his body
In Ireland, or win.

The army commander only speaks
French and Italian:
His army speaks either
English or Irish.
When he gives an order
His jowls bleach and blush
Like a turkeycock's dewlap.

Lieutenant-General Charles Chalmont,
Marquis of St. Ruth,
The Prince of Condé's disciple
In the music of war,
Jerks with spinal rapture
When a volley of musket fire
Splits his ear.

Picture his peregrine eyes,
A wife-tormentor's thin

Heraldic mouth, a blue
Stiletto beard on his chin,
And a long forked nose
Acclimatized to the sulphurous
Agony of Huguenots.

He keeps his crab-claw tactics
Copied from classical books
An unbetrayable secret
From his army of Irishmen.
He rides downhill to correct
A numerical mistake
In his plan's translation.

He throws up his hat in the air,
The time is near sunset,
He knows victory is sure,
One cavalry charge will win it.
"*Le jour est à nous, mes enfants,*"
He shouts. The next minute
His head is shot off.

THE WINNING SHOT

Mullen had seen St. Ruth riding downhill
And Kelly held a taper. "There's the Frenchman!"
Trench laid the cannon, a breeze curved the ball.

The victory charge was halted. Life Guards stooped down
And wrapped the dripping head in a blue cloak,
Then wheeled and galloped towards the setting sun.

Chance, skill, and treachery all hit the mark
Just when the sun's rod tipped the altar hill:
The soldiers panicked, thinking God had struck.

SARSFIELD

Sarsfield rides a chestnut horse
At the head of his regiment,
His mountainous green shoulders
Tufted with gold braid,
Over his iron skull-piece
He wears the white cockade.
A bagpipe skirls.

Last summer after the Boyne
When King James had run,
He smashed the Dutch usurper's
Waggon train of cannon
Benighted at Ballyneety.
Patrick Sarsfield, Earl of Lucan,
Commands the reserve today.

The saviour of Limerick knows
Nothing of St. Ruth's plan,
Not even that the battle
Of Aughrim has begun.
He has obeyed since dawn
The order to wait for further
Orders behind the hill.

He sees men run on the skyline
Throwing away muskets and pikes,
Then horsemen with sabres drawn
Cutting them down.
He hears cries, groans and shrieks.
Nothing he will do, or has done,
Can stop this happening.

MEN AT THE CASTLE

Comely their combat
    amidst death and wounds,
Romantic their disregard
    for cosmic detail:
The wrong kegs of ball
    were consigned to the castle,
Irish bullets too large
    for French firelocks.
A great stronghold
    became a weakness.
Till sunset they loaded
    muskets with tunic buttons
To fire on cavalry,
    squadron after squadron
Crossed the causeway
    and flanked their front.
Heroic volleys
    continued until nightfall:
They fell with no quarter
    when the battle was lost.

LUTTRELL

Luttrell on a black charger
At the rear of his regiment
Stands idle in a beanfield
Protected by a tower.
He wears a dandy yellow coat,
A white-feathered hat
And a gilded sabre.

When he hears the word spread
Along the line, "St. Ruth is dead,"
He retreats at a trot:
Leading his priding cavalry
To betray the humble foot:
Ten miles to a dinner, laid
In a mansion, then to bed.

PRISONER

Night covers the retreat.
Some English troops beating a ditch for loot
Capture a wounded boy. "Don't shoot!"

"What'll we do with him?"
"I'll work in the camp." "Strip him!"
Naked he kneels to them. They light a lamp.

"Pretty boy." "Castrate the fucker!"
"Let the papist kiss my flute."
"Toss a coin for the privilege to bugger . . ."

He cries like a girl. "Finish him off."
"No, keep him alive to be our slave."
"Shove a sword up his hole." They laugh.

A tipsy officer calls out:
"You men be on parade at eight.
I want no prisoners, d'you hear me? Shoot

The crowd we took, when it gets light.
We've no more food. Good night.
God knows you all put up a splendid fight."

4. After

THE WOLFHOUND

A wolfhound sits under a wild ash
Licking the wound in a dead ensign's neck.

When guns cool at night with bugles in fog
She points over the young face.

All her life a boy's pet.
Prisoners are sabred and the dead are stripped.

Her ear pricks like a crimson leaf on snow,
The horse carts creak away.

Vermin by moonlight pick
The tongues and sockets of six thousand skulls.

★

She pines for his horn to blow
To bay in triumph down the track of wolves.

Her forelegs stand like pillars through a siege,
His Toledo sword corrodes.

Nights she lopes to the scrub
And trails back at dawn to guard a skeleton.

Wind shears the berries from the rowan tree,
The wild geese have flown.

She lifts her head to cry
As a woman keens in a famine for her son.

★

A redcoat, stalking, cocks
His flintlock when he hears the wolfhound growl.

Her fur bristles with fear at the new smell,
Snow has betrayed her lair.

"I'll sell you for a packhorse,
You antiquated bigoted papistical bitch!"

She springs: in self-defence he fires his gun.
People remember this.

By turf embers she gives tongue
When the choirs are silenced in wood and stone.

THE REVEREND GEORGE STORY CONCLUDES
AN IMPARTIAL HISTORY OF THE
WARS IN IRELAND

"I never could learn what became of St. Ruth's corpse:
Some say he was left stript amongst the dead,
When our men pursued beyond the hill;
And others that he was thrown into a Bog:
However, though the man had an ill character
As a great persecutor of Protestants in France,
Yet we must allow him to be very brave in his person,
And indeed considerable in his conduct,
Since he brought the Irish to fight a better battle
Than ever that people could boast of before:
They behaved themselves like men of another nation.

"But it was always the genius of this people
To rebel, and their vice was laziness.
Since first they began to play their mad pranks
There have died, I say, in this sad kingdom,
By the sword, famine, and disease,
At least one hundred thousand young and old.
Last July alone, more execution was done
At Aughrim than in all Europe besides.
Seen from the top of the hill, the unburied dead
Covered four miles, like a great flock of sheep.

"What did the mere Irish ever gain
By following their lords into rebellion?
Or what might they have gotten by success
But absolute servitude under France?
They are naturally a lazy crew
And love nothing more than to be left at ease.
Give one a cow and a potato garden
He will aspire to no greater wealth
But loiter on the highway to hear news.
Lacking plain honesty, but most religious,
Not one in twenty works, the gaols are full
Of thieves, and beggars howl on every street.
This war has ended happily for us:
The people now must learn to be industrious."

LUTTRELL'S DEATH

Luttrell, Master of Luttrellstown
Sat in a gold and red sedan
The burden of a hungry urchin
And a weak old man
Barefoot on cobbles in the midnight rain,
Up torchlit quays from a coffee shop
Where after supper, the silver cup
Lifted, a fop had said,
"It's time to bury Aughrim's dead."

A poor smell of ordure
Seeped through his embroidered chair,
He slid the glass open for air,
Waved off a beggar groping at the door
And watched six black dray-horses cross
The river. "Let the traitor pass."
He felt his pocket full of pebbles
Which he used at Mass in straw-roofed chapels
To lob at little girls.

The chair slewed at his town house,
Flambeaus, footmen in place,
And plunked him down.
He'd sold his country to preserve his class,
The gutters hissed: but that was done
Twenty-six years ago, he said,
Had they not buried Aughrim's dead?
Standing under grey cut stone
A shadow cocked a gun.

No one betrayed his assassin
Although the Duke of Bolton
Offered three hundred pounds' reward.
The crowd spat on Henry Luttrell's coffin.
Eighty years after his murder
Masked men, inspired by Wolfe Tone,
Burst open his tomb's locks,
Lit a stub of wax
And smashed the skull with a pickaxe.

PATRICK SARSFIELDS PORTRAIT

Sarsfield, great-uncle in the portrait's grime,
Your emigration built your fame at home.
Landlord who never racked, you gave your rent
To travel with your mounted regiment.

Hotly you duelled for our name abroad
In Restoration wig, with German sword,
Wanting a vicious murder thrust to prove
Your Celtic passion and our Lady's love.

Gallant at Sedgemoor, cutting down for James
The scythe-armed yokels Monmouth led like lambs,
You thought it needed God's anointed king
To breathe our Irish winter into spring.

Your ashwood lance covered the Boyne retreat:
When the divine perfidious monarch's rout
From kindred enemy and alien friend
Darkened the land, you kindled Ireland.

At Limerick besieged, you led the dance:
"If this had failed, I would have gone to France."
When youths lit brandy in a pewter dish
You were their hazel nut and speckled fish.

A French duke scoffed: "They need no cannonballs
But roasted apples to assault these walls."
Sarsfield, through plague and shelling you held out;
You saved the city, lost your own estate.

Shunning pitched battle was your strategy:
You chose rapparee mountain routes to try
The enemy's morale, and blew his train
Of cannon skywards in the soft night rain.

Your king, who gave St. Ruth supreme command,
Mistrusted you, native of Ireland.
"Await further orders," you were told
At Aughrim, when your plan was overruled.

You stood, while brother officers betrayed
By going, and six thousand Irish died.
Then you assumed command, but veered about:
Chose exile in your courteous conqueror's boat.

"Change kings with us, and we will fight again,"
You said, but sailed off with ten thousand men;
While women clutched the hawsers in your wake,
Drowning—it was too late when you looked back.

Only to come home stronger had you sailed:
Successes held you, and the French prevailed.
Coolly you triumphed where you wanted least,
On Flemish cornfield or at Versailles feast.

We loved you, horseman of the white cockade,
Above all, for your last words, "Would to God
This wound had been for Ireland." Cavalier,
You feathered with the wild geese our despair.

BATTLE HILL REVISITED

Strangers visit the townland:
Called after wild geese, they fly through Shannon.

They know by instinct the sheepwalk
As it was before the great hunger and the exodus:

Also this cool creek of traitors.
They have come here to seek out ancestors.

They have read that the wind
Carried their forebears' gunsmoke, to make blind

The enemy, but nevertheless the Lord
Permitted the wicked to purify the good.

They know little about God
But something of the evil exploded by the word.

They are at the navel of an island
Driving slowly into well drained battleground,

To follow the glacial esker
By the new signpost to the credal slaughter,

Blood on a stone altar:
Seed, there should be seed, buried in a cairn.

If they listen, they may hear
Doubtless the litany of their houseled father.

Soon they locate the dun
Where St. Ruth spun the thread of his fatal plan:

They try to imagine
Exactly what took place, what it could mean,

Whether by will or by chance:
Then turn in time to catch a plane for France.

The God Who Eats Corn

1963

I

In his loyal garden, like Horace's farm,
He asks his visitors to plant a tree.
The black shadow of the African msasa
Squats among the lawn's colonial company.

In honour among watersprays that spin
Rainbows over cool English rose-beds
Hand-weeded by a pink-soled piccanin
The Queen Mother's cypress nods in a straw hood.

The trees are labelled: a chairman of mines
Gave this copper beech, that silver oak
Was trowelled by a Governor: great names
Written on tags, Llewellin and Tredgold.

Livingstone's heir presented this wild fig
From the burnt-out forest of Africa:
On its branches by moonlight a boomslang swings.
This Cape creeper has a cold blue flower.

As a son I choose the native candelabra:
Perched on an ant-hill, after years of drought,
From its cut spines a milky sap flows:
To my father I give this tree as a tribute.

His own plane-tree, brought by seed from Cos,
From shade where Hippocrates swore his oath,
Wilts in the voodoo climate, while gums
The trekkers imported have sapped the earth.

Under these trees, he wishes that indaba
Might avoid a blood-feud. Tree frogs crackle
Above the lily pond. A trickle of water
Like tolerance cannot cure the racist fever.

2

From his green study half-door he looks out
On the young plantation of his old age:
An ibis is perched on a cone hut,
Rain-birds croak in the citrus orchard.

Boys are sharpening pangas at the wood-pile:
Trailers approach, filling barns from the field
With limp tobacco to be dried by steam.
A Union Jack droops on the school flag-pole.

Hunkered on dust in kaffir quarters
With rickety babies, the sewing club meets
My mother bringing gifts through trellis doors
Frail as a lily in her straw sun-hat.

Such tinkle of bangles, such ivory teeth
Clacking, they gossip of clothes and clinics.
A child rolls a pram-wheel over the earth,
A cat is stalking the cooped-up chickens.

He drives to the store to collect his *Times*
And letters from home, tulip trees in flower,
Road-grit on his tongue, tobacco booms
A memory, hot wind raising a dust-choked roar.

He swims before breakfast in a patio pool
Sometimes recalling Atlantic light
Splashed on to hymn-books in a pitch-pine hall
Where his father preached. He prays at night.

At a carol service in the grading shed
He reads the lesson, joining trade with truth.
My knees remember his coconut mats,
The mesh of our duty to improve the earth.

3

"To do some good for this poor Africa"
Was Livingstone's prayer, but not the Founder's dream.
Towards gold and diamonds, the Pioneer Column
Trekked at the bidding of a childless millionaire.

They came with ox-wagons, claiming a treaty,
To the king's kraal, his great indaba tree,
With charming letters from Queen Victoria:
There the chameleon swallowed the black fly.

In dusty dorps they slept with slave-girls,
On farms they divided the royal herd.
In stifling mine shafts the disarmed warriors
Were flogged to work, their grazing grounds wired.

So now at white homesteads, the coffee steams
On creepered verandahs. Racial partners
Do not mix in wedlock sons and daughters.
The white man rides: the black man is his horse.

Brown bare feet slide softly over the tiles
Soothing the master, scrubbing his bath,
Folding his towels, timidly with smiles
Smoothing his pillow, and wincing at his wrath.

To each black, his ten acres for millet;
To each white, his three thousand of grass.
The gospel of peace preached from the pulpit;
From the hungry fields the gospel of force.

4

In a paradise for white gods he grows old
Cutting rafters out of the felled wood,
Baking bricks from the clay of ant-hills:
He plants the first rose on the burnt sandveld.

Thirteen years ago his books were unpacked
In the path of mambas, where nomads' fires
Lit stone age sketches on the walls of caves
And the sand was printed by lion spoor.
His Governor's helmet stowed in a teak chest,
He called back Homer after forty years'
Damp decay in the West of Ireland,
Retiring into sunlight on a thousand acres.

Trapped from tribes in their idle forest
Africans gathered to work for meal and poll-tax,
Their teeming women overcrawled by bony kids,
Calling him "Baas," grinning, hungry, diseased.

They built wicker-and-mud rondavels to sleep in.
Tractors invaded the elephant road.
A bore-hole was sunk. Cicadas at his fly-screen
Halted and schrilled. The kudu retreated.

He fed corn to his gang and cured fever.
Cigarettes sold in a London shop
Kept people stooped on his kopje alive.
Each year he felled more trees to plant a crop.

Between the auction floors and seed-bed sowing
First in a thatched hut he began a school.
The market rose and fell, drought followed flooding,
When the leaves ripened there were showers of hail.

Daily at dawn, they clang the plough-disc gong
That winds a chain of men through vleis and veld.
No boss-boy drives them with a sjambok's thong.
At dusk they come to class rooms to be schooled.

Children are chanting hymns, their lean bodies
Tropically sensual behind puritan desks,
From mealie plot and swamp of tsetse flies
Lured by the witchcraft of the god's mechanics.

A red-hot poker flowers in the playground,
A viper sleeps on the sand. The dry slate
Under the sweating palm is rubbed and scrawled.
They wait like logs, ready for fire and wind.

5

Tall in his garden, shaded and brick-walled,
He upholds the manners of a lost empire.
Time has confused dead honour with dead guilt
But lets a sunbird sip at a gold creeper.

His scholar's head, disguised in a bush hat,
Spectacled eyes, that watch the weaver's nest
Woven, have helped a high dam to be built
Where once the Zambesi was worshipped and wasted.

Sometimes he dreams of a rogue elephant
That smashed the discharged rifle in his hand:
Or reading, remembers the horns of buffalo,
The leopards he shipped to the Dublin zoo.

On the game-cleared plateau the settlers say
"This is our home: this is white man's country."
Dust-storms gather to hide their traces
Under boulders balanced in a smouldering sky.

6

They say, when the god goes, the rain falls,
Contour ridges burst, sweeping off crops,
The rafters crumble, trees shoot through floors,
And wind carves the fields into smooth dust-heaps.

The concrete cracks and the brown rivers bleed,
Cattle die of rinderpest, dogs with rabies
Bite their masters, the half-freed slaves are freed
But not into a garden that anyone remembers.

Now the old mopani forest is felled.
The settlers try to cling to their laagers,
Wire for a gunboat, dabble in gold shares,
Dream of silk flags and showers of assegais.

The trees that fail are soon devoured by ants.
Sundowners bind together a white crowd:
Some preach of partners, more sneer at the Munts
Getting cheeky, lazier than ever. He's bored.

While he prepares to fly to Ithaca,
The B.S.A. police hold rifle drill,
Pyres kindle under *Pax Britannica.*
He stays to build a club-room for the school.

At dusk on the stoep he greets ambassadors
From Kenya and Ceylon. The silver trays
Are lit by candles cupped in the flower borders.
Husks hang on his dry indaba trees.

Last thing at night he checks the rain-gauge
Remembering his father on a rectory lawn.
Thunder is pent in the drums of the compound.
He feels too old to love the rising moon.

3

High Island

AND POEMS OF

1968–1974

The calamity of seals begins with jaws.
Born in caverns that reverberate
With endless malice of the sea's tongue
Clacking on shingle, they learn to bark back
In fear and sadness and celebration.
The ocean's mouth opens forty feet wide
And closes on a morsel of their rock.

Swayed by the thrust and backfall of the tide,
A dappled grey bull and a brindled cow
Copulate in the green water of a cove.
I watch from a cliff-top, trying not to move.
Sometimes they sink and merge into black shoals;
Then rise for air, his muzzle on her neck,
Their winged feet intertwined as a fishtail.

She opens her fierce mouth like a scarlet flower
Full of white seeds; she holds it open long
At the sunburst in the music of their loving;
And cries a little. But I must remember
How far their feelings are from mine marooned.
If there are tears at this holy ceremony
Theirs are caused by brine and mine by breeze.

When the great bull withdraws his rod, it glows
Like a carnelian candle set in jade.
The cow ripples ashore to feed her calf;
While an old rival, eyeing the deed with hate,
Swims to attack the tired triumphant god.
They rear their heads above the boiling surf,
Their terrible jaws open, jetting blood.

At nightfall they haul out, and mourn the drowned,
Playing to the sea sadly their last quartet,
An improvised requiem that ravishes

Reason, while ripping scale up like a net:
Brings pity trembling down the rocky spine
Of headlands, till the bitter ocean's tongue
Swells in their cove, and smothers their sweet song.

LITTLE HUNGER

I drove to Little Hunger promontory
    Looking for pink stone
In roofless houses huddled by the sea
    To buy to build my own.

Hovels to live in, ruins to admire
    From a car cruising by,
The weathered face caught in a sunset fire,
    Hollowed with exility;

Whose gradual fall my purchase would complete,
    Clearing them off the land,
The seven cabins needed to create
    The granite house I planned.

Once mine, I'd work on their dismemberment,
    Threshold, lintel, wall;
And pick a hearthstone from a rubble fragment
    To make it integral.

LULLABY

for Shura

Before you'd given death a name
Like Bear or Crocodile, death came

To take your mother out one night.
But when she'd said her last good night

You cried, "I don't want you to go,"
So in her arms she took you too.

LARGESSE

There's a trawler at the quay landing fish.
Could it be one of the island boats?
Seldom we see them, but how glad we are.
They have a generous custom
Of giving away a box of dabs or fluke,
For luck, of course, for the unlucky poor.

And this is how it works:
Three tramps are walking down the docks
Casually, not hurrying, getting there
With enough drinking time to spare,
When a blue car fins along
And sharks the free fish-box.

Usually at this dusky hour
That car's owner
Is kneeling in the parlour with his wife.
If you go into their shop you hear
Nine decades of the rosary
And a prayer for Biafra.

Walking on Sunday into Omey Island
   When the tide had fallen slack,
I crossed a spit of wet ribbed sand
   With a cold breeze at my back.

Two sheepdogs nosed me at a stile,
   Boys chevied on the green,
A woman came out of a house to smile
   And tell me she had seen

Men digging down at St. Fechin's church,
   Buried in sand for centuries
Up to its pink stone gable top, a perch
   For choughs and seapies.

I found a dimple scalloped from a dune,
   A landing-slip for coracles,
Two graveyards—one for women, one for men—
   Odorous of miracles:

And twelve parishioners probing a soft floor
   To find what solid shape there was
Under shell-drift; seeking window, door;
   And measuring the house.

Blood was returning dimly to the face
   Of the chancel they'd uncovered,
Granite skin that rain would kiss
   Until the body flowered.

I heard the spades clang with a shock
   Inaugurating spring:
Fechin used plug and feather to split rock
   And poised the stone to sing.

He tuned cacophony to make
    Harmony in this choir:
The ocean gorged on it, he died of plague,
    And hawks nested there.

OMEY ISLAND

Was there a house or church for which these flesh-pink
Boulders were quarried but never used,
As if the builders had expired
Leaving random, irregular forms
Of a thousand years ago
To be dressed by vanished masons?

Or did no force but the sea
Split from solid rock these makings of ashlars,
And fling them above high watermark
To lie in confusion crying out
For hands to give them the grace of stonework
Lost in beehive cells buried under the sand?

With its loud mouth and sharp tongue the ocean
Explodes at the quarry-face of the shore
Without a notion of hearths, lintels, and tombstones,
Gathering more and more power
To rampage over the island, or disgorge
Enough raw granite to face a whole new town.

TRAVELLING MAN

What can have held him on the road so long?
A fair, a camp in a quarry, horses,
Pubs, or a girl bathing under a bridge?
He may have met with a crowd
From Tourmakeady or Kiltimagh.
A guard may have given him a summons.
Better not ask, if he turns up,
Just offer shelter and food.
Your door will never be his destination:
Sometime if he's passing he may knock.

WALLED UP

He danders down the forge lane
From the coastguard station to the shop
With a string bag for a message
They've told him to bring up,
And when he meets my garden wall
He asks, politely taking off his cap,
"How are the prisoners in Mountjoy Jail?"

DOUBLE NEGATIVE

for Tony White

You were standing on the quay
Wondering who was the stranger on the mailboat
While I was on the mailboat
Wondering who was the stranger on the quay

BALL'S COVE

Leaving her family at the lake
To dawdle over their antiquarian picnic,
She took Mr. Ball to the top of a cliff
On the ocean side, and said as a joke:
"The man I marry must prove he's brave.
Go out and stand on that beak of rock
And turn three times on your heel.
You'll have my money, if all goes well."

An hour later, she came back
Without Mr. Ball. She looked terrified.
"I tried to talk him out of suicide.
He asked three times for my hand.
I told him I hadn't made up my mind,
And then he threatened
To throw himself over a ghastly cliff.
Before I could stop him, he'd gone."

The coroner helped. "A sad accident."
The boatman kept silent,
Well paid
By those grand people who came from abroad.
But a lobster fisherman said:
"She pushed him off,
I can prove it. I was near the cove
Hauling pots, and I heard her laugh."

Why weave rhetoric on your voice's loom,
Shuttling at the bottom of my garden
In meadowsweet and broom?
Crepuscular, archaic politician,
It's time to duck down,
Little bridegroom.

Why draft an epic on a myth of doom
In staunchly nailed iambics
Launched nightly near my room?
Since all you need to say is *crex*
Give us lyrics,
Little bridegroom.

Why go on chiselling mottoes for a tomb,
Counting on a scythe to spare
Your small defenceless home?
Quicken your tune, O improvise, before
The combine and the digger come,
Little bridegroom.

CORNCRAKE

Petty boss of a ditch
Why so much energy and such a boring song?
Surely your mate must be tired of hearing
How little you have to say
And how often you repeat yourself
Through the small hours of the night
While she is silently sitting on her nest
And producing your offspring
O yes, you're a hero to distract the attention
Of everyone away from her significant
Silent creation
By compelling us to listen to your cant
Though you really can't help it
You'd prefer to sing like the lark
But the only flying you can manage
Is involuntary migration
Trailing your fleshy feet behind you
Just clearing meadow and cornland
Dipping with relief into the nearest drain
Instead of upwards into the sun
And never where you're likely to be seen

COPPERSMITH

A temple tree grew in our garden in Ceylon.
We knew it by no other name.
The flower, if you turned it upside down,
Looked like a dagoba with an onion dome.
A holy perfume
Stronger than the evil tang of betel-nut
Enticed me into its shade on the stuffiest afternoon,

Where I stood and listened to the tiny hammer-stroke
Of the crimson coppersmith perched above my head,
His *took took took*
And his *tonk tonk tonk*
Were spoken in a language I never understood:
And there I began to repeat
Out loud to myself an English word such as *beat beat beat*,

Till hammering too hard I lost the meaning in the sound
Which faded and left nothing behind,
A blank mind,
The compound spinning round,
My brain melting, as if I'd stood in the sun
Too long without a topee and was going blind,
Till I and the bird, the word and the tree, were one.

His finger smells of rubbings out and sharpened lead.
She's teaching him to write.
The table stands in little bowls of fluid
To keep down cockroach and termite.
Above them sags a ceiling cloth
Stained by civet cats prowling in the roof.
A punkah fans them, while he copies *God Is Love.*

What are words made of? Squiggles, lines, dots.
Sweat spoils the page.
If he writes well, she'll give him a bicycle
To ride round the compound while his brother walks.
For silly mistakes, she'll rap his knuckles.
John's dusting the Crossley's khaki hood.
Let's go to the breakwater! Let's go to the Officer's Beach!

"Run out and play." Appu's cooking curry for lunch.
He stands under a flowering temple tree
Looking up at a coppersmith perched on a branch:
Crimson feathers, pointed beard.
All day long it hammers at a single word.
Is it bored? Is it learning?
Why can't it make a sentence, or break into song?

JURORS

—Why did he kill her? Jealousy, anger, drink?
There's always more to it than what you hear.

—It had to happen, it was coming to her,
Unfortunate girl, since the day she was born.
He used to work as a turfcutter:
The man she left him for drove a van in town.

—Why are they taking so long to arrest
If they saw him follow her out of the hall,
And found her shoe on the road, her body pressed
Head first into a stream behind a wall?

—They've sent away his boots to be analysed,
And a few ribs they found of her chestnut hair.

PAT CLOHERTY'S VERSION OF *THE MAISIE*

I've no tooth to sing you the song
    Tierney made at the time
        but I'll tell the truth

It happened on St. John's Day
    sixty-eight years ago
        last June the twenty-fourth

The Maisie sailed from Westport Quay
    homeward on a Sunday
        missing Mass to catch the tide

John Kerrigan sat at her helm
    Michael Barrett stood at her mast
        and Kerrigan's wife lay down below

The men were two stepbrothers
    drownings in the family
        and all through the family

Barrett kept a shop in the island
    Kerrigan plied the hooker
        now deeply laden with flour

She passed Clare and she came to Cahir
    two reefs tied in the mainsail
        she bore a foresail but no jib

South-east wind with strong ebb-tide
    still she rode ... this way ... that way
        hugging it ... hugging it ... O my dear

And it blew and blew hard and blew hard
    but Kerrigan kept her to it
        as long as he was there he kept her to it

Rain fell in a cloudburst
　　hailstones hit her deck
　　　　there was no return for him once he'd put out

At Inishturk when the people saw
　　The Maisie smothered up in darkness
　　　　they lit candles in the church

What more could Kerrigan do?
　　he put her jaw into the hurricane
　　　　and the sea claimed him

Barrett was not a sailor
　　to take a man from the water
　　　　yet the sea claimed him too

At noon the storm ceased
　　and we heard *The Maisie* had foundered
　　　　high upon a Mayo strand

The woman came up from the forecastle
　　she came up alone on deck
　　　　and a great heave cast her out on shore

And another heave came while she drowned
　　and put her on her knees
　　　　like a person would be in prayer

That's the way the people found her
　　and the sea never came in
　　　　near that mark no more

John Kerrigan was found
　　far down at Achill Sound
　　　　he's buried there

Michael Barrett was taken
　　off Murrisk Pier
　　　　he's buried there

Kerrigan's wife was brought from Cross
    home to Inishbofin
        and she's buried there

This well is holy but looks foul.
I clean it seven times a year,
Shovelling quicklime in the shade.
It fills mysteriously dark red.
Once I found a drowned wheatear
And once an old ram's skull.

How does it rise on top of a hill
And why is it never clear?
By miracle, tradition said:
Instead of springing, the rock shed
A slow continual tainted tear
Since Brian Boru's fall.

It was named by St. Gormgall,
Hermit, lion, poet, seer,
And king's confessor. When it bled
He knew his penitent was dead.
He saw millennial daybreak tear
Unwinding from its spool.

Even in drought it will not fail
But bless or curse. Don't interfere!
A bigot sledged the crystal bed:
Next day he shot his son in the head
Wild fowling. I cut outlets there
To keep it drinkable.

High Island pivots on this pool.
If a fly walks on the water
All's well with your friend abroad.
It quenched St. Brendan's thirst on board
When he touched here to pray before
Setting out for Hy Brasil.

Around the random horseshoe wall
I helped a mason to repair,
Pennies, fish-hooks, pins corrode.
A thousand years this carved stone stood
Beside the well, giving it power
To comfort or to heal.

THE READING LESSON

Fourteen years old, learning the alphabet,
He finds letters harder to catch than hares
Without a greyhound. Can't I give him a dog
To track them down, or put them in a cage?
He's caught in a trap, until I let him go,
Pinioned by "Don't you want to learn to read?"
"I'll be the same man whatever I do."

He looks at a page as a mule balks at a gap
From which a goat may hobble out and bleat.
His eyes jink from a sentence like flushed snipe
Escaping shot. A sharp word, and he'll mooch
Back to his piebald mare and bantam cock.
Our purpose is as tricky to retrieve
As mercury from a smashed thermometer.

"I'll not read any more." Should I give up?
His hands, long-fingered as a Celtic scribe's,
Will grow callous, gathering sticks or scrap;
Exploring pockets of the horny drunk
Loiterers at the fairs, giving them lice.
A neighbour chuckles. "You can never tame
The wild duck: when his wings grow, he'll fly off."

If books resembled roads, he'd quickly read:
But they're small farms to him, fenced by the page,
Ploughed into lines, with letters drilled like oats:
A field of tasks he'll always be outside.
If words were bank notes, he would filch a wad;
If they were pheasants, they'd be in his pot
For breakfast, or if wrens he'd make them king.

ARDILAUN

Ocean blue light
Breaking through
Four days of mist
And calculated solitude
Is lifting up
White and mauve parasols of angelica
Briefly to celebrate.

It strikes the black
Schist of a beehive cell
As long roots
Resurge
Causing graves to open
And ferns to poke new heads
Through cracks in penitential crosses.

Beaming down
It liquefies and pours
Through a wrecked chapel's doorway
On a patch of ox-eye daisies
Little egg-yolks
Little suns
Redeeming more than a year lost

Probing the darkness
Of a friend's life
For gleams that never broke through.
When I leave the island
Tomorrow at sea under thick clouds
Gloom will lift in the afterglow
Of unpolluted light.

NOCTURNE

The blade of a knife
Is tapped gently on an oak table
Waves are sobbing in coves

Light bleeds on the sky's rim
From dusk till dawn
Petrels fly in from the ocean

Wings beating on stone
Quick vibration of notes throats tongues
Under silverweed   calling   and calling

Louder cries cut the air
They rise from a pit
Complaints are retched up and lost

A solo tune
Is dying with passion
For someone out there to come quickly

Come back!   Come back!
I'm here   here   here
This burrow   this wall   this hole

Ach! who kept you?   where've you been?
There   there   there
It's all over   over   over

SUNUP

The sun kisses my eyes open:
Another day of wanting you.
I'd like to kiss your eyes again,
No comfort now in being alone.

Is she delighting you in bed
In her caravan on a cutaway road?
Does the sun give you the same kiss
To wake you, with her at your side?

I kiss you both, like the sun,
I kiss your hands and your feet,
Your ears and your eyes,
Both your bodies, I bless them both.

Do you feel this when you make love?
Do you love her as I loved you?
Will you let her steal all you have
And suffer her to leave?

Meet me today! We'll find a wood
Of blackthorn in white bud:
And let me give you one more kiss
Full of sun, free of bitterness.

Thunder in the patanas. He's falling off a cliff.
Every branch he catches breaks.
Down he hurtles, counting . . . one . . . two . . . then wakes
In the nick of time. His heart pounds with relief.
It's Nanny's afternoon off.
He untucks his mosquito net
And shakes the fear of scorpions from his shoes.

Hours to go, nothing to do but wait.
A tom-tom roars at the Temple of the Tooth.
He peeps at the bathroom coolie rinsing a pot,
Picks up his cat
And saunters out on the upstairs nursery verandah.
"Would Marmalade die if he fell from this height?"
A bullock-bandy creaks past the compound gate.

"Why don't you try it?" his brother says.
"Cats have four feet to land on: they're not like us."
He hugs the warm purring bag
Of muscle, fur, and bone.
"Suppose it kills him?" "I dare you to do it."
The boy holds his pet over the green balustrade
And lets go.

The legs fly out like an X. Marmalade pancakes
And lies dead still on the lawn.
A wanderoo gibbers in the crown of a royal palm.
"Look! he's alive: I saw him twitch."
They rush downstairs
In time to see the cat
Vanish near a snake-hole under a jasmine hedge.

That night he walks to the chair with long wooden arms;
Whisky glass, tobacco pouch, crossword puzzle, pen;
To own up like a gentleman.
Scent of cartridges ejected from a shotgun,

Glint of pince-nez, mosaic frown.
The hand with a gold signet ring bends him down,
A lion rampant on a little hairy finger.

Out in the jungle beyond the fire-fly net
Poochies are biting Marmalade, sucking his blood.
Tuck up tight.
"I'm not going to kiss you tonight, naughty boy."
Do all experiments go phut?
Early in the morning kitchen coolies shout.
Marmalade walks in purring . . . four unbroken feet.

FIREBUG

He's tired of winding up the gramophone
Halfway through "Three Little Maids,"
And waiting for a rickshaw to return from the bazaar.
The monsoon teems on the compound.
A coolie, splitting coconuts on an iron spike,
Stoops to wring the rain out of his loin-cloth.
The boy picks up a box of matches.

His little sister comes from the nursery holding a doll.
"Give me that!" "What for?"
"I want to set it on fire." "You wouldn't dare."
"I will if you help me."
She puts the doll on the floor. He strikes a match
And holds it gingerly under the pink legs.
The girl screeches like a cockatoo.

The fire bursts into song,
Eats the doll, sticks out its tongue, stands up
Gyrating like a crimson top: then dies.
Burnt celluloid leaves a guilty smell.
The girl cries over the ashes, "Give me back my doll!"
"An angel took it to heaven, didn't you see?"
The devil needs thrashing with a shoe.

Straining my back
Seven times I've lifted you
Up to my thighs

There are men
Who've put you sitting
High on their shoulders

It looks as if you'd been
Lopped
Off the top of a column

Then used as a quern
Kicked around
Buried

An archaeologist
Taped you
And wrote you down

He said
You're an oblate spheroid
Does it matter?

Whoever carved you
Gave you all
The time in the world

STORMPETREL

Gypsy of the sea
In winter wambling over scurvy whaleroads,
Jooking in the wake of ships,
A sailor hooks you
And carves his girl's name on your beak.

Guest of the storm
Who sweeps you off to party after party,
You flit in a sooty grey coat
Smelling of must
Barefoot across a sea of broken glass.

Waif of the afterglow
On summer nights to meet your mate you jink
Over sea-cliff and graveyard,
Creeping underground
To hatch an egg in a hermit's skull.

Pulse of the rock
You throb till daybreak on your cryptic nest
A song older than fossils,
Ephemeral as thrift.
It ends with a gasp.

GALLOWS RIDDLE

Hangman   In I went, out again,
Death I saw, life within,
Three confined there, one let free:
Riddle me that or hung you'll be.

Tinker   Five maggoty sheep I stole
Tangled me on the gallows tree,
Now my tongue must riddle me free:
A nest of birds in an old man's skull.

A candle was burning in the caravan
Parked where three roads forked beside a mound
Of broken bottles near a market town.
A woman was tottering home
With a bundle of children's clothes and a loaf of bread
After closing time.
A camp fire in the ditch was dying out.

She peeped into the tent and heard her children breathe.
A snipe drummed on the moor.
The wagon door was bolted. Why had he shut her out?
A bantam cock on the axle tree
Opened his eyes and crowed.
She peered through a smirched pane of glass,
Fell on the ground and screamed.

A candle was burning beside the bed
Spilling wax on the table, guttering in the draught.
A man was kneeling naked
Over a naked child
Offering her his penis to play with like a toy.
Hearing a noise outside
He quickly stubbed the candle flame with his thumb.

A whippet chained to the axle growled.
A child woke in the wattle tent, and cried "Mammy!"
The caravan leaned silently as a tombstone
Over the woman lying prone on the mud
Weeping. What should she do?
The breeze tugged at a skirt hung on a thorn to dry.
She staggered down the road to fetch the Guards.

You take off your new blancoed shoes at the temple door.
She wraps them in tissue paper,
Humming her favorite bars of *Pomp and Circumstance*.
Lightly your feet slip, feeling the cool marble floor.
"Stop showing off! Remember where you are!"
Flambeaus, tom-toms, flageolets, incense.
Devil-dancers, with a clash of cymbals, begin to dance.

They hobble and sway above you on bamboo stilts:
Crocodile, panther, jackal, monkey, toad:
Tongues hanging out, paddy-straw hair, boils and welts
On bums with tails, torsos gummy as rubber trees,
Jungle-fowl feathers glued on thighs.
Each bears the spots or sores of an incurable disease.
Copper bells clang on elbows, ankles and knees.

They block the corridor you've got to pass. Their sweat
Steams like monsoon rain on a path of dust.
Coconut cressets, carried by almost naked men,
Burn with a sickening fume.
"Nan, I'm thirsty. Can't we go home?"
Your mouth is as dry as pith on a mango stone.
You turn and bury your head in her old green gown.

She smarms your hair, tightens the knot in your silk tie:
Takes you out on a high cool balcony
Freed from the ant-hill crowd.
Huge howdahed elephants lumber out of a wood,
Trapped under jewelled caparisons. Gongs and floodlight.
"When I grow up, will you let me marry you?"
"By the time you're old enough, I'll be buried in Timbuktu."

A monk hangs a garland of temple flowers round your neck.
Tea planters chatter and smoke.
"How did the Tooth fit in Buddha's mouth?"
"It must be a tiger's. Nobody knows the truth."

Can't you see which elephant carries the holy relic?
Pain jabs your heart. Poison! You almost cry.
Doesn't she realize: Won't she believe? You're going to die.

A pigeon's blood ruby sparkles in Lady Weerasirie's nose.
Hum of malarial mosquitoes.
Worse and worse the pain. "Can we go home soon?"
At the temple door you put on your shoes.
A priest in a saffron robe is watching you. "Goodbye."
Mind you don't step on a scorpion.
Full moon, tree-frogs, fire-flies: a brutal jungle cry.

Your throat's burning. Will there be time to reach home
And call Dr. Chisel? Look, here's a traveller's palm.
She shows you the place to sink
The point of an ivory pen-knife you won in a race:
A dark olive leaf-sheath curving out of a dry old stem.
If you die, can you be reborn? Try!
Even if the water of the tree is poison, drink!

WOMAN MAROONED

They wanted to believe in miracles.
When they found that after three days
Marooned on High Island
The poor woman had borne a child
Their faith was confirmed.
Angels had come down from heaven and acted as midwives
Bringing a white garb to wrap up the baby.
The woman herself said she'd felt no fear
And was never hungry or thirsty.
The time had passed like a dream wrapped in fog.
The terrible loneliness
The cruel birth-pains
Suffered without any human company
Were all wiped away
The moment she fell from the rock
Fainting with relief into her rescuers' arms.

A shoulder of rock
Sticks high up out of the sea,
A fisherman's mark
For lobster and blue-shark.

Fissile and stark
The crust is flaking off,
Seal rock, gull rock,
Cove and cliff.

Dark mounds of mica schist,
A lake, mill, and chapel,
Roofless, one gable smashed,
Lie ringed with rubble.

An older calm,
The kiss of rock and grass,
Pink thrift and white sea-campion,
Flowers in the dead place.

Day keeps lit a flare
Round the north pole all night.
Like brushing long wavy hair
Petrels quiver in flight.

Quietly as the rustle
Of an arm entering a sleeve,
They slip down to nest
Under altar stone or grave.

Round the wrecked laura
Needles flicker
Tacking air, quicker and quicker
To rock, sea, and star.

4

Care

MOONSHINE

To think
I must be alone:
To love
We must be together.

I think I love you
When I'm alone
More than I think of you
When we're together.

I cannot think
Without loving
Or love
Without thinking.

Alone I love
To think of us together:
Together I think
I'd love to be alone.

CARE

Kidded in April above Glencolumbkille
On a treeless hill backing north, she throve
Sucking milk off heather and rock, until

I came with children to buy her. We drove
South, passing Drumcliff. Restless in the car,
Bleating, she gulped at plastic teats we'd shove

Copiously in her mouth. Soon she'd devour
Whatever we'd give. Prettily she poked
Her gypsy head with hornbuds through barbed wire

To nip off pea-tops, her fawn pelt streaked
With Black Forest shadow and Alpine snow.
I stalled her wildness in a pen that locked.

She grew tame and fat, fed on herbs I knew
Her body needed. We ransacked Kylemore
To bring her oakleaf, ivy, and bark to chew.

I gutted goatbooks, learning how to cure
Fluke, pulpy kidney, black garget, louping ill:
All my attention bled to cope with her.

No commonage to roam unfenced, no hill
Where she could vanish under a dark cloud
To forage with a puck-led flock: but the shrill

Grind of small children bucketing her food,
Yelling across a yard. Out in a forest
She would have known a bad leaf from a good.

Here, captive to our taste, she'd learnt to trust
The petting hand with crushed oats, or a new
Mash of concentrates, or sweet bits of waste.

So when a child mistook a sprig of yew
And mixed it with her fodder, she descried
No danger: we had tamed her instinct too.

Whiskey, white of egg, linseed oil, we tried
Forcing down antidotes. Nothing would do.
The children came to tell me when she died.

This root of bog-oak the sea dug up she found
Poking about, in old age, and put to stand
Between a snarling griffin and a half-nude man
Moulded of lead on my chimney-piece.
It looks like a heron rising from a pond,
Feet dipped in brown trout water,
Head shooting arrow-sharp into blue sky.

"What does it remind you of?" she wanted to know.
I thought of trees in her father's demesne
Levelled by chainsaws;
Bunches of primroses I used to pick
Before breakfast, hunting along a limestone lane,
To put at her bedside before she woke;
And all my childhood's broken promises.

No, no! It precedes alphabets,
Planted woods, or gods.
Twisted and honed as a mind that never forgets
It lay dead in bog acids, undecayable:
Secretively hardening in a womb of moss, until
The peat burnt off, a freak tide raised
The feathered stick she took to lure me home.

Bare feet she dips across my boat's blue rail
In the ocean as we run under full white summer sail.
The cold spray kisses them. She's not immortal.

Sitting in her orchard she reads "Lady Lazarus"
Aloud rehearsing, when her smallest child lays
Red peonies in her lap with tender apologies.

She walks by Lough Mask in a blue silk gown
So thin the cloudy wind is biting to the bone
But she talks as lightly as if the sun shone.

SHELTER

Girl with a sheaf of rye-straw in your arms
How much you carry from a loaded trailer
Parked at the door in a stray sunny shaft
At the tail end of summer, deep into the barn
To store for thatch, if ever we get the weather
Or the time, before winter sets in, how much
You help me, child, in the hour after school,
Hour of your release, face wet with tears
That well up out of a cruelty done to you,
Bruise marks around your lips, a speechless harm,
How much you help me to make the dark inside
Glitter with sheaves bound firm to keep out storm.
Hear how they rustle as we lay them down:
Their broken heads are thrashed clean of grain.

SCYTHE

In a small meadow between outcrops of granite
        above a church that's buried in sand
                on Omey Island
An old farmer, who has lived here all his life
        without a machine, is teaching
                at my request
A tinker whose tribe has never owned land
        how to hold and handle
                a scythe.

They are cutting hay for the tinker's goats
        in the driest summer, Joeen says,
                since 1921
When tinsmiths were welcome on remote farms
        before plastic made them pariahs
                people hoped
The county council would settle decently in houses
        but not in our parish, heaven help us
                not next door!

As I watch them, a glint of sun catches
        the edge of a scythe upturned
                for the whetstone.
Be careful of your fingers, Paddy Oilcake!
        You know how to sharpen a knife
                to cut tobacco
But not this primordial blade of the farmer
        you might quit travelling
                to become.

How easy it looks! How relaxed the expert's
        arms and shoulders oscillating
                on the pivot of hips,
Heel of the scythe not scraping the ground
        as it sweeps back and forth
                sprung like a timepiece

Advancing swathe by swathe over warrior grasses,
cocksfoot and crested dogstail,
their plumes laid low.

NICHES

Lovers I've lost are sleeping in the house I've left
To live alone in a cave with two glass entrances,
A skylight in the roof over a chair that broods
At the bottom of a well of sunshine on clear days,
Or a pit of night kept warm by a peat fire
When hailstones jitter, as now with a northerly gale
Squalling through cracks in my costly new shell:
While two calm urns of white Cycladic clay
Stand silently still in niches I drew last summer
In the random warm granite of my chimney breast.
A woman threw them lovingly, glazed them in tears,
Fired them one sleepless night, and put them here to stay
For ever. Now she's dismantled her wheel and gone.
Niched above my head I'll keep her bone-ash jars.

She wades through wet rushes,
Long autumn grass,
Over rusty barbed wire
And stone walls that collapse,

With a black rubber torch
Flickering on and off,
After midnight, to reach
A shed with a tin roof.

She lifts away door boards—
O sweet herbal hay!
Her beam dazzles birds
She can't identify.

Timorous wings in wormy rafters
Flap to get out.
Then she spots in a light shaft
A red boot unlaced.

The flock's tremor increases
In her torch's coop.
Where is he? She sees
A white arm sticking up.

How much it hurts me to tidy up when all my papers are
    heaped on the desk in a three-month mess,
To regain control of this drift of days I've lost in my
    passion for building in granite,
And face the bills I must pay by leaving the house
    that has cost me too much to enlarge,
Where I passed the time too quickly preparing a place for
    the future to work within soundproof walls,
So never had a moment in the present for writing about
    the moments that were passing away:
How much it hurts to see the destruction that all good
    building, even the best, must cause,
Not only the hedges that had to be first cut down
    before the foundations were dug,
But deeper cuts through veins in the mind that carried
    the blood of memory through the brain:
How much it hurts me to have neglected all this summer
    the friends whom I might have seen,
But for my mad obsession of building more rooms
    to entertain them in time to come:
Because these times are apt to elude us, we die, or our
    friends drop dead before we can say
I'd love you to see and enjoy the house whose construction
    has kept us entirely apart.

Sheep like to graze on headlands
High up looking down on a raging sea.
It makes me dizzy to watch
An old ewe
Leaning over the edge to reach with her black mouth
A tuft of grass fine as hair.
I'd have to crawl there clutching frail stems.

How many of the flock fall
Dashed on to rocks or drowned in surf
To satisfy a peculiar hunger.
No soft herb
Pleases them as much as the spikes of gorse.
If I were their shepherd
I'd put them to fatten in a small safe paddock.

Smoky as peat your lank hair on my pillow
Burns like a tinker's fire in a mossy ditch.
Before I suffocate, let me slowly suck
From your mouth a tincture of mountain ash,
A red infusion of summer going to seed.
Ivy-clumps loosen the stonework of my heart.
Come like a wood-pigeon gliding there to roost!

I float a moment on a gust sighing for ever
Gently over your face where two swans swim.
Let me kiss your eyes in the slate-blue calm
Before their Connemara clouds return.
A spancelled goat bleats in our pleasure ground.
A whippet snarls on its chain. The fire dies out.
Litter of rags and bottles in the normal rain.

Your country and mine, love, can it still exist?
The unsignposted hawthorn lane of your body
Leads to my lichenous walls and gutted house.
Your kind of beauty earth has almost lost.
Although we have no home in the time that's come,
Coming together we live in our own time.
Make your nest of moss like a wren in my skull.

TONY WHITE

1930–1976

Growing, he saw his friends increase
Their incomes, houses, families,
And saw this growth as a disease
Nothing but unpossessive love could cure.
Possessing nothing, he was not possessed
By things or people, as we are.
His granite chimney breast
Warmed friend or stranger at its open fire.
There was no air
Too foul for him to breathe, no pit
Too dark to enter, yet
His very breathing made the foul air pure,
His presence made the darkest day feel clear.

He lived at the hub and not the rim
Of time. Within himself he moved
Deeper towards dangerous ideas he loved
To moot with bodily risk:
Flying too close to the sun's disk,
Sailing at night over a coral reef,
Ghosting a thief's life.
Since he's gone
No words of mine can rivet him to one
Role of some forty-nine he used to play
For pleasure more than pay.
Because his kind of love taught me to live
His dying I forgive.

TONY WHITE AT INISHBOFIN

1959

With a lobster pot for a chair
And a fishbox for a table
He'd sacrificed a plausible career
On the London stage to live near
The sea in a bare room
Far from home
To become on the lips of islanders a fable.

In an old pair of black jeans
Threadbare though tautly darned
By himself needling with a woman's patience
Buckled in a looted Hun's
Eagle and swastika belt
Disguised he felt
Reborn as a fisherman whose craft he learned.

From an off-white Aran sweater
Knit by his neighbour's wife
His dark face opened like a long love-letter
That makes a forlorn reader
Revive with a gust of hope
While he moused rope
For crayfish traps with a horn gutting knife.

Through small panes of cobwebbed glass
Across a limewashed stone sill
He hauled in shoals of riffled sun to please
Only a few friends like us
Because it was his style
To play as well
Carrying a creel on his back or Coriolanus.

BOOKCASE FOR THE
OXFORD ENGLISH DICTIONARY

All the words I need
Stored like seed in a pyramid
To bring back from the dead your living shade
Lie coffined in this thing of wood you made
Of solid pine mortised and glued
Not long before you died.

Words you'll never read
Are good for nothing but to spread
Your greater love of craft in word and deed,
A gift to make your friends' desires succeed
While inwardly with pain you bled
To keep your own pride hid.

CIRCLES

These are rocks he loved when he was alive
And how alive he was, like the sun this afternoon
Making mica gleam on the cold face of granite
And giving walls a long shadow across the grass
In the dead of winter, when he'd come from abroad
Like the sun emerging now from behind that cloud
To flood this dark lake water with golden light,
So that I still believe in him as in the sun,
And expect him to reappear as winter passes,
The telephone ringing some stormy night, his voice
Calmly announcing the day he's planning to cross
Back into our lives with so much news to tell
Of where he has been since he died, though I know
It's only a dream, so vivid it makes me cry
"Tony, it's you! What the hell made you play
This trick on us? Thank God you're alive and well!"
Which cannot be, though the sun breaks through
All the clouds on the lake where I cast his ashes
And a heron rose from these rocks like a ghost
In three wide circles ascending who knows where.

Two swans take off from the wind-ruffled
Water of a pond below my hexagon
And a heron glides down to poise on a rock
In a clump of reeds and waterlilies.

With his long grey neck stretched out he sees
All the eyes in the country
That are looking at him, including
Mine through the lenses of binoculars.

It scares and compels him to change his perch
To a half-rotted stake that no longer
Supports a barbed wire fence
Between neighbours at loggerheads.

In a dark liquid circle he turns
The power of his vision on the silt
Of decades muddying the bottom
Where fish he dreams about lie embedded.

Now I can only see the top of his head
Far off pointing down. Could this be the bird
That soared from a rock in lake water
As our friend's ashes broke out of your pot?

Up from trawlers in the fish dock they walk to my house
On high-soled clogs, stepping like fillies back from a forge
Newly shod, to wake me at sunrise from a single bed
With laughter peeling skin from a dream ripening on mossy
Branches of my head—"Let us in quick!"—and half naked
I stumble over books on the floor to open my door of glass
To a flood that crosses the threshold, little blue waves

Nudging each other, dodging rocks they've got to leap over,
Freshening my brackish pools, to tell me of "O such a night
Below in the boats!" "We can't go home! What will they say?"
Can I think of a lie to protect them from God only knows
What trouble this will cause, what rows? "We'll run away
And never come back!"—till they flop into black armchairs,
Two beautiful teenage girls from a tribe of tinkers,

Lovely as seals wet from fishing, hauled out on a rock
To dry their dark brown fur glinting with scales of salmon
When the spring tide ebbs. This is their everlasting day
Of being young. They bring to my room the sea's iodine odour
On a breeze of voices ruffling my calm as they comb their long
Hair tangled as weed in a rockpool beginning to settle clear.
Give me the sea-breath from your mouths to breathe a while!

SEA HOLLY

Thrives upon sand where no other plant can live
Close to high water mark on haggard shores,
And crops up briefly in summer wearing stiff
Armour embossed with mauve and sapphire flowers.
All the rest of the year it spends underground
In stupefying torpor. How can it raise
Enough energy to rise above the sand
Piled over it by waves, and open its eyes?
Like yours, the colour of hurt, they want to hide
Until in a blaze of blue spikes they explode.

QUAYS

Waiting for the sun to rise in Syracuse, New York,
the snow to melt and a term of grief to pass,
I think of boys who sailed with me
from deserted quays at Rosroe and Cleggan,
Inishturk and Renvyle, Boffin and Shark,
long grown distant from tidal heaves
that broke over our bows
at the Leahy Rocks, Cuddoo, and Carrigmahog,
having wives and children to look after
with cars and television,
no more hand-hauling anchor chains, as when
for sheer love and small money
we toiled with rods and hand-lines
far out kedging for pollock on shoals by day,
then cabined in the dark, our warps made fast
to bollards on a slippery fishgut-tainted quay,
where the sea gave an odd suckling sigh
as it ebbed from the dock
and our hull, bruised against a wall of barnacles,
used to groan as we came to rest.

ARSONIST

The summer visitors have gone.
Rain blathers at the glass.
He drifts alone
On the soundwaves of his vacant house.

So firm his tongued and grooved oak floors!
By his building he's possessed.
His dark teak doors
Creak as they close him in his past.

Each random stone made integral
Has bonded him with debt.
All he can feel
Is a dying to get rid of it.

With craft to burn, how could he use
Control to lose control,
To spark a blaze
Spontaneous and elemental?

Fire would transmute his home in hours
To a foetiferous void,
A mould that flowers
Gravid with fronds of gutter lead.

Turning a stone house into seven figures
Transported him to money's clean cold alp
To hang-glide on a market's thermal rigours
Learning new ways to corner, hedge or scalp.

Turning a copper nail that tightly gripped
A green slate on his roof to daily bread
Made him afraid to eat when sterling dipped
And meat cost more than door-locks or sheet lead.

Turning a life's work into stocks and shares
Converted him to shirk the tears and shocks
Of love, rid of laborious household cares
And freed him to buy sex on piers and docks.

Turning old granite walls to bars of gold
Amassed his fears of sudden falls in one
Commodity. When all his wealth was told
It filled a vault with bone-dry speculation.

Turning his home into a foreign room
Replete with art to beat inflation chilled
His heart to zero. In that ice-bound tomb
He housed immortal seed unsowed, untilled.

Blocking the way to get behind the house
To climb crooked stone steps to see the view
A huge grey granite boulder lay. With you
To help, I'd shift the obstacle with ease.

Was it a mass-rock blessed in penal days
Better left undisturbed? Too near the wall
It made our bedroom weep. Too flat to roll
It caught a bulldozer between two trees.

A stalwart mason told us to use fire
And water. One calm Sunday we piled coal
To heaven. Then doused the hot slab from a pool.
Not a seam cracked. Instead, we'd fouled the air.

Chagrined, we tried digging a deep wide pit;
Eased down the bald obtruder; buried it.

Those years ago, when I made love to you,
    With fears I was afraid you knew,
    To grow strong I'd pretend to be
A boy I'd loved, loving yourself as me.
I played his part so open-eyed that you
    Believed my artful ploy was true.
    To show I'd nothing false to hide
And make you feel the truth of love I lied.

The love of truth made me confess, and died
    Exposing my hermetic guide,
    A youth found loitering in the mart
Of memory's torn-down inner city heart.
I feel betrayed by dead words that decide
    If head or tail be certified.
    Dear girl, come back and take a new
Lover in me, let him make love to you.

How can I comfort you? What can I say?
You seem so far away, though near me now,
Sedated in that iron bed
Behind a curtain I'm afraid to draw:
With languished head
Propped on a pillow, mute and weak.
Would it be better not to speak?

Do you remember the day
We drifted west of Cleggan Bay
In the slack of tide, a fish on every hook:
The crossed lines and the lost
Leads, and seagulls scrawling around the mast
That listed while waves yeasted over a rock:
The gutted pollock gasping on our deck?

At least your poetry will stay unblurred.
Stuck with needles in this ward,
No peasant shoulders to support your feet,
You lie and fret. Work incomplete.
Tubes in your throat. And this is you,
Who put flesh into words that can't renew
The life you lavished making them ring true.

5

Sri Lanka

AND POEMS OF

1985–1992

MANGOES

A colourful boy in a Star Wars tee-shirt
and a saffron batik sarong
tightrope walking along a mango tree's
top branches
figurine fired in the midday sun
is raining down on the parched red earth
glittering hard green fruit.

Seeing you focus binoculars
to pick him out
as a black-headed oriole of Ceylon
for your notebook's cage
he shins down the trunk embracingly,
to bring you a gift of mangoes robbed
with a tartly negotiable smile.

*

Where are you going? A terracotta road
Winds from a tower-block on a tourist beach
Around a lake dyed bottle-green with garbage
Of a foetid shanty slum. It turns your head.

Out of the ditch a pearly grinning guide
With Tamil pride in his bold English speech
Springs up to fasten on you, like a leech,
Charm that could make your skin feel deified.

You can hide nothing on this scathing track
Which puts on trial your childhood. You are lost
For want of a poor abandoned native boy
To love and father, giving him the luck
Showered on you here in your imperial past
With soaring confidence, great guilt, much joy.

Soon after you heard the genial warden call
    "Nimal!" a slim dark boy with a sweet
    Cup to offer came in his bare feet
    From work in a spice garden: so beautiful
His face, not yet street-wise, with institutional
    Small scars, black irises watering to meet
    A tall white guardian, that in withering heat
    You swallowed more than nectar: all in all
You found the cast off natural child you'd come
    Flying back fifty years to seek, who'd sprung
    From bible mould of a mission compound left
To soldier on when your people sailed home:
    Whom fathering by word of mouth you bring
    To love, leaving his native tongue bereft.

Couched in cement and whitewash at my feet
Four lions cast a monumental grin
On cricket pitch, kovil, and minaret,
Bo tree with beggars cringing from the sun.

High on the clashing horns of trishaw, van,
Minibus, juggernaut, I'm equipoised,
Reborn in bronze, a Singhalese businessman
Who died in the king's uniform disgraced.

"Shot as a lesson for all traitors to come,"
The Town Guard captain who refused to shoot
Rioters of my own race, I feel calm
Redressed in loyalty buttoned to the throat.

Going up a martyr's moonstone steps to power
When mobs loot, burn, and slaughter, I inspire.

1985

Being nearly heart-shaped made me seem a ham
   On early spice trade navigators' charts
   Tinctured with cinnamon, peppered with forts,
To be eaten up under a strong brand name
Like Taprobane, Serendip, Tenarisim—
   Copper-palmed lotus island slave resorts—
   And I succumbed to lordly polished arts
That cut me down to seem a white king's gem,
A star sapphire tear-drop India shed
   On old school maps, a lighthouse of retorts
Flashing from head to head. My leonine blood
Throbbed wildly when resplendent freedom came
   Mouthing pearl tropes with Pali counterparts,
Exalted, flawed; and made me seem as I am.

The flowers of the ironwood
Last for a day.
Opening at sunrise
They fall when the sun goes down.

Their little white flags
With yellow hearts
Flutter in a state
Of carnival and terror.

Yesterday's petals
Lie beheaded on the ground.
There are buds in hiding:
Tomorrow these will explode.

Above the low scrub jungle
Seething in hot air
The young leaves turn
Transparently blood-red.

A king cobra demon
Stays hoodwinking on top.
The ironwood grows high
Exuding festivity.

January 1989

A half-ripe cataract in my left eye
                              makes the world
              look like a damaged old master

My right eye has a view
                              of unvarnished clarity
              through a new synthetic lens

At night my left eye
                              sees the numinous
              glory of the moon blurred

My right eye pictures it
                              hanging from a parachute
              by minuscule threads of light

from *The Mirror Wall*

KASSAPA

Perhaps the king, whose name evoked the sun,
Riding his elephant, under a pearl umbrella,
Through parched rice-fields on the dry zone plain,

Had seen this rock aspiring from the earth
To penetrate the clouds loafing in heaven:
And put five hundred of his virgin brides,

Dressed in cascades of jewellery, to make
A splash on the summit, and entice the gods
To cast their semen on the ground as rain:

Then shone here, as the god of wealth, supreme
In rice and gems, going about on three legs,
Devising arts to give the gods sublime

Erections that would last: broad galleries
Of golden girls the rock itself embraced
Inside a wall whose mirror caught their souls:

And sheathed the rock-head in a lion mask
To father a strong race, out of whose mouth
At festivals he made great fountains pour.

You who remain
fresh on the rock
may think:

'In our endless youth
surviving here
we've never met

a man we could love
who did not die
when slain.'

Beyond looking brilliant
Have they nothing in mind?
You men call them faithless.
Didn't your gold brushwork
Make them what they are?

A woman wrote this for women
Sealed in the rockface
As gems on show to the crowd.
Their star sapphire eyes
Look far too bright to be touched

From Hunagiri Temple
I've come with all I possess:
Needle, fan, begging bowl,
And my robe as a novice.

A person much talked about
Lives up in that cave, whoring.
Be wakeful in thought:
Guard the door of hearing!

She spreads a broad grin
Round a soul she's devouring.
Terrible thing to have seen.
I can't stop shuddering.

The wet monsoon
   came to us in a thunderstorm
      bursting with relief.

Clay pots and brass bowls
   overflowed with drips
      from leaks in broken roofs.

Hundreds and thousands
   of trees like birthday cake candles
      were lit in a flash and blown out.

Tuna and seer-fish
   got whirled into the sky
      and landed among spice gardens.

A curlew felt cheated
   and left the country
      filing a wretched complaint.

From the summit of parched hills
   waterfalls roared
      like tomtoms beaten in temples.

In our cots at night we crowed
   when firefly swarms kept bringing
      miniscule buds of light.

You, with your eyes half closed
   as a nymph of the Lion Rock
      stirred up these airs.

If we'd known the secret
   of sapu flowers at your fingertips
      would it have helped?

As a woman I'll gladly
    sing for these women
   who are unable to speak.

You bulls come to Sigiri
    and toss off little lovesongs
   making a big hullabaloo.

Not one has given us
    a heart-warming sip
 of rum and molasses.

Maybe none of you thought
    we women could have lives
 of our own to get through.

Sigiriya, 11 January 1987

Early this morning
   I walked on the ramparts
    and came across lotuses,

A playful flotilla
   becalmed on the moat
    hauling white sails down,

As warm rain was falling:
   each leaf collecting in the palm
   of my hand as a child

Drops that scatter and split
   like mercury: held very still
   they pool and unite.

    ★

We were lightly fanned
   by a friendly wind
      with a scent of jasmine

Around an octagonal pond
   where the king could recline
      in his pleasure ground

Backed by a huge rock lingam
   watering a lotus bed
      whenever it rained:

We could see our reflections
   Blossoming from the mud
      in fragrant, flamboyant air.

      *

The freshness we found
   near the cobra hood cave
      on white marble steps

Going up to the clouds
   came as kindness from someone
      who usually makes our blood boil:

All the better when we stood
   above the gallery walkway
      between rock and mirror wall,

And watched a transparent
   drop-curtain of rain
      coming down from the gods

By drip-channels grooved
   in the overhanging cliff:
      and saw the violent green

Jungle of the country
    from this high point of love
        diffused through a purifying screen.

They came here, looked around, and went,
With this karmic picture
Etched upon their minds.

But they couldn't stop their hands
Wanting to touch
As they climbed and stumbled down.

You salacious people,
Keep your hands off the images!
Don't go giving each breast a rub.

The Price of Stone

1981–1984

For Dennis O'Driscoll

FOLLY

I rise from a circle standing on a square
And cock my dunce's cap at the firmament
Keeping my ignorance tapered to a clear
Sugarloaf point above the dark green ferment.

A lord's pride made me to relieve the poor
With heavy work lifting my spire, and the rich
With light step ascending my gazebo stair
To admire the land they owned and wish for more.

My form is epicene: male when the gold
Seed of the sun comes melting through my skin
Of old grey stucco: female when the mould
Of moonlight makes my witch-pap cone obscene.

My four doors bricked up against vandals, still
Tumescent, scrawled with muck, I crest the hill.

LEAD MINE CHIMNEY

Pointlessly standing up to make a pointed
Remark on a skyline everyone can see
Not puffing smoke out any more, disjointed
By age, I speak of cut stone symmetry.

Remember when you look at my cold grey stack
I took the heart from oakwoods to smelt ore,
Made people richer, poorer. Now I lack
The guts to pour out sulphur and hot air.

When you've poked your head inside my bevelled flue,
Inhaled a sooty chill of hollowness,
You'll know I've lost the fury to renew
The furnace at my root, all that foul stress.

Clearly I'll go on uttering, while I may,
In granite style, with not a word to say.

PORTICO

A dark headland hangs in a beady noose
Of mercury vapour across a bay of mud.
All night, solitary shadows of men cruise
My concrete cloister, ghosts questing blood.

I perch on rocks by the cineritious sea
Fossilized in decay: no painted porch
For a stoic mind, no shore temple of Shiva,
But a new kind of succursal, deviate church.

My spumy grotto's hooded devotees,
Sucked in a black hole that the sea has scoured,
Perform on flutes groping, mute melodies
With a seedy touch of ithyphallic art.

My hymns are hog-snorts, squealing bottle-glass
Screwed underfoot, a wave's foghorn caress.

My duty done, I rose as a Doric column
Far from at home, planted to reach the sky;
A huge stake in the crossed heart of a glum
Garrison city overlooked by my blind eye.

One-armed on a cold square abacus to rule
The waves, I never controlled the verminous
Poor beggars round my plinth, schooled to rebel.
I was loved well as a tramway's terminus.

Who cares, now, what good masons carved my four
Sea victories in granite from Golden Hill?
When masked men cracked my head off, the blast wore
Red, white, and blue in a flash of puerile skill.

Dismasted and dismissed, without much choice,
Having lost my touch, I'll raise my chiselled voice.

WELLINGTON TESTIMONIAL

Needling my native sky over Phoenix Park
I obelize the victory of wit
That let my polished Anglo-Irish mark
Be made by Smirke, as a colossal spit.

Properly dressed for an obsolete parade,
Devoid of mystery, no winding stair
Threading my unvermiculated head,
I've kept my feet, but lost my nosey flair.

My life was work: my work was taking life
To be a monument. The dead have won
Capital headlines. Look at Ireland rife
With maxims: need you ask what good I've done?

My sole point in this evergreen oak aisle
Is to maintain a clean laconic style.

GEORGIAN TENEMENT

The high court of dry rot, after a long
Unreportable session behind airtight doors,
Has mouthed a verdict. Rafters know what's wrong.
Death and cremation. Up with my soft floors.

I've got to be rebuilt. Some new, banal
Office block is decreed to fill my place.
The whores under the trees by the canal
Increase their turnover while I lose face.

Young lovers of old structures, you who squat
To keep my form intact, when guards arrive
With riot gear and water gun, we cannot
Under such tonnage of cracked slate survive.

Would that your free hands in my spongy wood
Could cure fungosity, make my flaws good.

GYM

Vice-regal walls dominate the back street
Where men, succumbing to my spurious name
For body culture, enter in retreat
From words that shame, to act a heartless mime.

Discreetly couched, taking no verbal risk,
Ingled in clutches masked by sauna steam,
Nude club members, immune from women, bask
In tableaux mixed with musak, cocaine, jism.

See how my fabric, full of cock and bull,
Grotesquely free, though ruled by symmetry,
Lays you in some small penetralian cell
To come to grief, past all immunity.

The powers that be, served covertly by AIDS,
Strip to the bone your skin-deep masquerades.

When driven to explore a strange blind alley
First clambering footloose up a speckled hill
You gambled on rare views of infilled valley,
Blossom of Chinese tang on a thorny grill.

Coming to speculate, you stayed for good:
Your fortune in the gold market of whins.
Avuncular pines admonished you to brood
On dark tale ends with woodcut colophons.

A spirited father walked barefoot to Rome:
A son died sniffing glue. Nobody lasted.
Well finished as rifle bolts at the Somme
My door-locks made you feel safely invested.

Grey granite cropped up an archaic head
To check your feet, your line of living dead.

ICE RINK

Reflections of a spotlit mirror-ball,
Casting a light net over a pearl pond
In oval orbits, magnify my haul
Of small fry at a disco, coiled in sound.

On anticlockwise tracks, all shod with steel,
Initiates feel exalted; starlets glide
To cut more ice with convoluted skill
Practising tricks that lure them to backslide.

Their figure-carving feet have chased my skin
With puckish onslaught. Gloss they vitiate
For pure fun, when they joust through thick and thin,
Vanishes under frost, a hoar-stone slate.

Midnight, my crushed face melts in a dead heat:
Old scores ironed out, tomorrow a clean sheet.

CARLOW VILLAGE SCHOOLHOUSE

Much as you need a sonnet house to save
Your muse, while sifting through our foetid pits
Of blighted roots, he needed my firm, grave
Façade, to be freed from bog-dens and sod-huts.

Such symmetry he gained from me, you got
By birth, given his names. Twenty poor scholars,
Birched if they uttered Irish words, he taught
To speak like you, faults notched on wooden collars.

We faced the cross-roads four square. Where I stood
Is void now, so be fair. Not forced to sip
The cauldron soup with undying gratitude,
Would *you* have chosen to board a coffin-ship?

All you've seen is his proud clean signature
As a wedding witness that worst famine year.

ROOF-TREE

After you brought her home with your first child
How did you celebrate? Not with a poem
She might have loved, but orders to rebuild
The house. Men tore me open, room by room.

Your daughter's cries were answered by loud cracks
Of hammers stripping slates; the clawing down
Of dozed rafters; dull, stupefying knocks
On walls. Proudly your hackwork made me groan.

Your greed for kiln-dried oak that could outlast
Seven generations broke her heart. My mind
You filled with rot-proof hemlock at a cost
That killed her love. The dust spread unrefined.

To renovate my structure, which survives,
You flawed the tenderest movement of three lives.

RED BANK RESTAURANT

Was it a taste for black sole on the bone
Brought you two down from your mountain farm one night
To meet that Faustian guest, whose writing shone
In her sight, eating devilled prawn by candlelight?

Le sang du pauvre, he quipped, gulping more wine
You'd pay for, squandering the blood-money received
From her pilot brother's crash. Richly malign
Elevation of the hostess he'd conceived.

His cruiser eyes, when not nailed to her cross
By mother wit, fled exiled through the bar:
Soon to be reconciled, screened by clear glass,
As he smiled at his cold brilliance mirrored there.

All you could think was that your sloe hedge field
Would need spike-harrowing for a better yield.

LITTLE BARN

It's not my place to speak more than I must
Whether of bloodstock, interest rates, or corn.
She feels enclosed inside a lacquered nest
Of Chinese boxes, sealed from your concern.

I've been converted to increase the rent
Between us, cornered in a stable yard;
Spruce enclave, heavenly views; a fortress meant
To keep out southern storms; flint cobbles tarred.

Those Russian dolls her infant son and yours
Breaks open as a blue-eyed Williamite
He puts together again without more tears.
Your customs are so strange we can't unite.

She moulds the clay and fires the waterpot
He balances, authorised by you or not.

I should have done this, that, and all those things
Goodwill intended when I was designed
To end the poor land's hunger. Failure brings
Catches that slip through nets too close to mind.

Men stood me up here, promising that I'd be
Their godsend: ocean would provide more food.
The green earth should have married the grey sea,
But fell foul of her storms, her moody tide.

Attached by strings of warps to my stone head,
Fine wooden craft came, to be overcome
By torpor. Keels took root in silt of seabed,
Ribbed frames rotted in a frayed hemp dream.

You played in these hulks half a century ago.
What did you think you might do? Now you know.

BIRTH PLACE

I'd been expecting death by absentee
Owner's decay, or fire from a rebel match.
Too many old relations I'd seen die
In the same bedroom made me scared to watch.

Between her cries, I heard carts trundling books
Gone mouldy to a bonefire in the yard.
Wild bees in my roof were filling up their wax
Hexagonals from our lime-trees, working hard.

A boy led a pony round and round a small
Hedged pond, pumping spring water for her use.
And then your birth-cry came, piercing through wall
Behind wall. The sun transfigured all of us.

It shone like honey on doorsteps of brown bread.
The August evening kissed her worn out head.

Her face is gone from me. Only her voice
Will spring to mind as water underground
Near an abysmal swallow-hole, the place
Where toddling after a ball you almost drowned.

A dirty rascal egged you on, then dug
His foot in your back. A giant grabbed your hair
Standing on end, with a strong gardener's tug
To root you out, and shake you in pure air.

You breathed her love away like a dandelion head
In my field of vision, looking all day long
For your duck, wandering astray. Is she dead?
Gorged by the fox? You made such a sad song.

Listen to me! She's coming back. O look!
Here, with seven ducklings. You could write a book.

I'm steaming home, ploughing your peace of mind,
With the bow-wave poise of a duchess coaching through
Her deep blue shire; buoyantly waterlined;
Brass port-holes burnished by my lascar crew.

Dolphins precede us, playing for good schools
With somersaulting skills. Petrels astern
Writhe in our screwed up wake. Obeying the rules
You're learning to spin rope quoits, turn by turn.

Child, when you've sailed half way around the world
And found that home is like a foreign country,
Think how I've had to keep an ironclad hold
On your belongings, not to lose heart at sea.

The gong is ringing. Here comes your ice-cream.
There's more to mind than raising heads of steam.

We're putting off the day they'll pull us down
And fell our prickly monkey-puzzle tree
That lords it over the heather in our garden
Standing up to the wind and rain defiantly.

I love the watercolours curlews paint
With iodine on a quill down a glen's throat;
Deplore the country's poor mouth complaint;
Wear fuchsia tweed, an ancient ivy coat.

Can't you eat rabbit? Does it make you sick
To find your father's gun-shots in your meat,
Or touch a trout he's caught? You ought to like
Wearing an Eton collar; you look sweet.

All the roots that would pack inside a tea-chest
Came home when we retired from the Far East.

FAMILY SEAT

Clouds make me look as though I disapprove
Of everyone. You know that grim, grey face
Of limestone cut by famine workmen. Love
Is never allowed to show it rules the place.

But love I took from a ruling family,
And gave them back a wealth of lovely things:
As a trout river talking with propriety
Through cockshoot woods, bailiffed by underlings.

Their silver knives adored their crested forks.
Blue-veiny hands, like yours, kept my clocks wound
On endless landings: others did good works
Like typing braille. High walls surround my land.

They've all been buried in their name-proud vaults.
Paraplegics live here now, and love my faults.

RECTORY

My porous rock foundations can't keep down
Rising damp from arcane rheumatic springs
That creep up walls. Wet plaster makes him frown,
As when her black dogs leap up, licking things.

She lets them loose. He's choked by a dog-collar.
Time's silver chain is hung on his clean breast.
They sniff at holy orders, flung in choler:
Scenting her cling of lavender, feel blessed.

He carpets boys like you for playing with fire.
Bitches on heat can make mixed marriages.
You're lock-jawed by his chin-wag. Jubilee year,
Have you no higher thoughts than dog-rampages?

Her pups retrieve your first poem: a dead duck
Stuffed with bay-leaves. Page after page they pluck.

Bog-brown glens, mica schist rocks, waterfalls
Gulching down screes, a rain-logged mountain slope
With scrawny pine-trees twisted by mad gales,
They see from my ball-yard, and abandon hope.

Wild boys my workshops chasten and subdue
Learn here the force of craft. Few can escape
My rack of metal, wood, thread, hide: my screw
Of brotherhood: the penny stitched in a strap.

Podded in varnished pews, stunted in beds
Of cruciform iron, they bruise with sad, hurt shame:
Orphans with felons, bastards at loggerheads
With waifs, branded for life by a bad name.

One, almost hanged in my boot-room, has run free
Dressed as a girl, saved by a thieving gypsy.

Describe a gate lodge like a dragon's mouth
Taking in boys and parents with a grin;
Then spitting out the parents. Iron teeth
Close when the last proud vintage car has gone.

Start counting days of terminal homesickness
Minus the love of those who left you here.
Draw six parallel lines cut quick across
Two flaming circles. Be prepared for war.

Stand up, our youngest new boy, what's-your-name!
Your uncle ate a wineglass in his mess
At Woolwich, and Dobbs major a live worm
Washed down with ink. Prove you're no cowardly ass!

Open your mouth wide, and with one bite take
The candle burning on this tower of cake!

CANTERBURY CATHEDRAL

What building tuned your ear for poetry? Mine,
You remember, trained your childhood voice that filled
My quire with a sharp sound. You poured in my fine
Keyed vaults the grains of song my stonework milled.

When Canon Crum took you to climb dim stairs
That spiralled into my cranium, did you dream
You'd found my brain, with its treadmill, slow repairs,
Refacing a gargoyle, splicing an oak beam?

Now, you've come back, not to sing the *Te Deum*
In my nave, but to retrieve from your song's ground
The love you gave me then. Above the triforium
It soared to reach martyrs in stained glass crowned.

"Nine o'clock on a clear night, and all's well",
You heard, as you fell asleep, with my curfew bell.

CHOIR SCHOOL

Our mother church raised me on Kentish flint
Foundations dug in the Black Prince's day.
Two lily-white boys from dissolute Ireland,
You starred with your brother in our passion play.

How could you reach Mr. Knight's perfect pitch,
Control his organ-stops, ten hands, four feet?
Good God! How could you score without a hitch
His music sheets, braced for a lofty treat?

"Glorious things" your ruff-necked voices rang
In Mr. Poole's purple passage through Caen stone.
One Easter, despite Hitler's bombs, you sang
Our new Archbishop to St. Augustine's throne.

You shared my dormer view. A fiendish power
Rained fire on us: God spared Bell Harry Tower.

One year at home under our flagging roof
During the war, learning and love made peace.
As with a cottage weaver's warp and woof
Your heart and mind were shuttled into place.

Verbs conjugating in our Pleasure Ground
Held the past present in contiguous time.
Here was the Bower of Bliss, painlessly scanned.
You found the oldest trees were best to climb.

In neutral Ireland, our walled demesne
While tilting you towards knight-errant books
Groomed you to mount war-horses to gain
Rewards beyond our laurels and our oaks.

A peeled rush, dipped in tallow, carried light
From the dark ages, kissing you good night.

GATE LODGE

Two Irish yews, prickly green, poisonous,
Divide my entrance, tapering in trim gloom.
Old rookery buildings, pitch-pine resinous,
Wake up shell-shocked, welcoming you back home.

Barefoot a child skips from my hearth to touch
The wrought obsequious latch of lip-service;
Taking you in, between double gates, to reach
Beyond the ruts your mother's peerless place.

I face my forebear's relic, a neat sty
That hovelled with his brogue some grateful clod
Unearthed by famine; and I hear go by
Your souper choir school voice defrauding God.

Pigeon park, pheasant wood, and snipe bog lie
Within my scope ... your shotgun territory.

MILFORD: EAST WING

Stiff to open, needing a gentleman's grasp
Or a strong young maid's, my hall door, tight in its frame
Of wood at the long lime avenue's end, would gasp
With delight if callers of the old calibre came.

No judder shook my back door's ease of pulling
Lame ducks in; tinkers with babies, diseased and poor,
For a bite to eat; mockery of the cook killing
A rat with a poker on the foul scullery floor.

If it heard a piano playing, or psalms being sung,
A goat used my study door to butt in, and lie
Sniffing your mother's foot, for devilment bleating
Low notes that made your voice break on high.

My postern had to be nailed up, ivy-bound,
To keep the farmyard out of the pleasure ground.

CARLYON BAY HOTEL

Designed for luxury, commandeered to house
Your bombed out school, under Spartan rule I live
In a Cornish idyll, with high and mighty views:
Royal blue channel, Phoenician tin-veined cliff.

Don't you know there's a war? It's why you're here
Debarred from girls, a pup among top dogs.
Home is ninety days off, and you've no future
Hunting hares over treacherous Irish bogs.

Wing-collared Milner scholar, don't forget
Your gas-mask, ration book, identity card.
My buckthorn wood hears inklings in the black-out.
Uncle Jack's killed in Africa. Work hard!

Your voice is breaking. Kneel, and be confirmed
By Truro's hands of clay. Do you feel transformed?

Fear makes you lock out more than you include
By tackling my red brick with Shakespeare's form
Of love poem, barracked here and ridiculed
By hearty boys, drilled to my square-toed norm.

Yet ushered in, through my roll of honour voice,
Cold baths in winter, field days on Bagshot Heath,
Poetry gives you unconscripted choice
Of strategies, renaissance air to breathe.

Your father's brother fell in the Great War,
Your mother's fell in this. You ate our salt.
Should you plead conscience when called up next year
Their greater love would find the gravest fault.

Weren't you born to command a regiment?
How selfishly you serve your own heart's bent.

Going up a flight of stone at seventeen
In wartime, wearing thin your plodding soles
On coupons by degrees, you pass between
Dons' billowing gowns and chapel aureoles.

Brought to your knees by genuflectory prose—
C. S. Lewis, stoking the clinkered grate
Of lost causes, keeps you on your toes—
You're taught to criticise, but not create.

That numinous cloud of jovial pipe-smoke round
His Tudor head, wraps you tongue-tied as bells
Before V.E. Day, taking steps to sound
The blissful city fraught with private hells.

A fellowship of bowls on the cloister lawn
Do you miss, old man? You slipped up, going down.

CONVENIENCE

The public servant of men's private parts,
Plain clothed in the underground below Eros,
With white glazed stalls, and see-through mirror arts,
I plumb our language empire's omphalos.

Your profane oracle, I speak through a crack
In a mental block, going far back to the year
You stood here, epicentred on the shock
Of gross accusation, quaking at words like queer.

I watched you face an absurd firing squad
Unbuttoning uniforms. I, too, had lost
My primal sense in the promiscuous crowd.
Detected, blackmailed, judged, you paid the cost.

A life sentence, ambiguously imposed,
Props you behind all kinds of bars, exposed.

Look where I'm stuck the wrong side of Lough Fee:
Bad road, no neighbours, in the squally shade
Of a bleak mountain. Yet you took to me
When young. What made you seek my solitude?

Did you need my poor virgin concrete shell
No family cared to live in, just to write
Poetry, worshipping my waterfall,
Abased in loneliness by lust at night?

Still flowing steadfast in a flagstone cleft
Of stunted alders clinging on, it pours
With resonant gravity, bringing the gift
Of widespread raindrops crafted to great force.

Hearing that strong cadence, you learned your trade
Concerned with song in endless falling, stayed.

The young have redressed my slated history
Nailed to this wild coast in the famished past
On a deep ocean inlet, and restored me
As their last outpost of folksong and feast.

Mackerel swim through my windows at high tide.
You blotted a blank page of lyrical youth
With epic faults in my loneliest interlude,
Hooked here in boyhood on the Tír na n-Óg myth.

Didn't you follow that exiled Austrian
Who stood on my murky lane with a walking-stick
Drawing diagrams for the birds to explain?
Sea-urchins mocked him with folkloric tricks.

He left, in my turf-shed rafters, a small sign
To question all our myths. . . . *Dear Wittgenstein.*

My deeds are tied up in a family trust
Embracing a salmon river, nightly poached
By sweep-nets, to her ladyship's disgust,
Her private reaches tortuously encroached.

Tucked behind rhododendron palisades
I sheathe you with your mate in a dug-out gloom.
You lumber home at dawn to cast-iron beds,
Trickle of spawn-tanks through a shuttered room.

I'm living in the past, among record fish
She hooked on badger-hair, played to her gaff,
Carved for blue-blooded guests on a Ming dish,
And immortalised with a game-book epitaph.

While watching, do you poach? With sovereign guile
Beyond reproach, she only kills in style.

KYLEMORE CASTLE

Built for a cotton king, who loved the view
Unspoilt by mills, improved by famine's hand
That cleared away people, petrified I grew
Grotesquely rich on mountainous, poor land.

To last for ever, I had to be faced in stone
Dressed by wage-skeletons; a spindly pile
Of storm-grey turrets that defended no one,
And broke my maker, with his fabricated style.

Coming from church to hold her usual place
On Christmas nights, wheeled to the dining-room,
His wife's corpse embalmed in a sealed glass case
Obeyed his command in the brandy-lit gloom.

Now, my linen-fold panelled halls retain
In mortmain his dark airs, which nuns maintain.

Never to be finished was the work he'd planned
When he restored my site, rebuilt the wreck
Of burnt thatch and disbonded walls he'd found
Bleak on a hillock between the ocean and a lake.

A weird huckster had lodged here in the past
Who could cure all diseases; he used to talk
To a dark rock split by lightning; the last
Night he walked out there he never came back.

Always your friend looked forward to being alone
In my raw stone skin, with a wren and a mouse
That crept through random masonry, while a swan
Nested on an island he saw through raindrop glass.

Never to be finished was the life you'd planned
To spend near him. How well he'd understand!

For donkey's years I've stood in lashing rain
Unbudgingly, casting a fish-hawk eye
On dock-tied hookers. How could we regain
Lost native custom tourist cash would buy?

Snug in my torporific trammelled air
Of a dream village roped to a lifeless quay,
I can help you play with an old craft, but your
Ten-feathered jigs will get fouled up at sea.

What brings you back to me, having said goodbye
To bullhead shillings in my hand-carved till,
Unless to greet, reflected through my dry
Distillery, the dead friend whose glass I fill?

Why drown so carefully with moss-hung chain
On sound moorings? Rig me. I'll entertain.

Unused in your desk drawer lies my brass key
To tongue-tied stonework, musky fossil tunes
You've locked away. Come back, not to unmask me
Word for word, but to make me sound in my ruins.

I rose from a desecration of corbelled cells
And hermits' graves in a sea-walled sanctuary:
Rock taken over by great black-backed gulls
Saluting each other *Sieg Heil*, claiming the sky.

Sink no more mineshafts to bring up fool's gold
With fever. You can't give every spall's lost face
A niche in the anchoretic oratory. Hold
My still-room as a rock-pipit's nesting place.

Bring oil to unseize my lock. The lode of ore
To smelt will sound like a fault: wheatear, shearwater.

Three watchful openings of clear plate glass
Give you command of a stormy desolate view
From my hilltop sundial cell as you look across
Dunes, rocks, and sea to islands west of Omey.

Six random walls round one all-purpose room
Of calm rupestral concentricity,
With a smell of yeast-bread flowering, enwomb
Your pride in the hermit hut you made of me.

Oak bed, a hundred books, a staunch teak door
And the Twelve Pins of your childhood I include.
No need for you to write. Sun and moon pore
Over curled up fly-leaves, brilliantly intrude.

Flood-tide, closing the strand, comes to embrace
Our isolation. Blue arms interlace.

From derelict huts of Cleggan rock I grew
To look most natural here, though I began
Strangely: your Breton stone design drawn through
A London architect's Dunfermline plan.

For thirteen years this perfect place to write
Creviced you in my Galway garden bond:
Green Cumbrian slates letting in attic light;
Slieve Donard heather's white cross-border stand.

Why did you sell me? Did you feel trapped here,
Compelled in cold blood to exuviate
My hard pink shell? A Dublin auctioneer
Hammered you free to grow articulate.

Our union was split level. Now I'm used
To keep old men with infant minds amused.

COTTAGE FOR SALE

If you have lost someone you tried to own
Buy me instead. I need to be possessed
For more than seaside weekends: stone by stone
Personified, gaps filled with interest.

Build on my real estate; squander in style
Your passion for belongings; ditch your thought.
Restore old thatch, strip off asbestos tile.
Shape me with love I can't escape, being bought.

Bring children here, and spoil them with my view
Of ocean; burnet roses growing between
Granite outcrops. Let barbed wire renew
Your landbonds. Plant me with a windproof screen.

I'm on the market. Hear my brochure's cry:
Vacant possession, sewn up endlessly.

My red half-door opens. The mother of nine
Looks at the tip-head where we've stuck, and curses.
"Whenever he took us out of one misfortune
He brought us into another that was worse."

How many stitches I got, sheltering those two
With their hatchets! They'd slash the skewbald cob
To tread down gaps in hedges we'd go through.
Mostly it was each other's joy they'd rob.

I'd rock like a cradle when they'd start to brawl
Over bottles. Storms did less harm than the pair of them
Spigoting my barrel-top. No luck at all,
No calm until cuckoo slipped into Jerusalem.

If I'm not scrapped sooner, or sold for the price
Of a drink, she'll burn me when the old lad dies.

A horse trotting loose, or a cow might stray
By my comatose door. Nobody passed a remark,
All the years I desquamated in decay
Tumorous on the bog-road in the priestly dark.

Now there's a new earth-mover's claw to feed,
The jaws are chewing me over. Neighbours are scared
Because they've heard I'll house a lazy breed
Of verminous, ditch-born tinkers, if repaired.

Let them come, with banners of torn tee-shirts hung
From smashed windows, looks that will turn the milk
Of decent mothers sour. Let my stone sing
With tongues of cant. Let the saintly village sulk.

How can they move me if I keep folk bound
Like spavined jennets padlocked in the pound?

CHALET

No shelter on this site when ocean gales
Assault my cabbage-green school weatherboards:
I stand rebuilt on ground made up of shells,
Dock silt and worms, clay pipes and bog orchids.

Nuns moved me here to install itinerants
With seven children, lost at a district court,
Dumped for their parents' fault in stone-walled convents.
My joinery cramped the family it restored.

Makeshift immobile home, need I be stilted,
Unstable? When my aerial blows down
They kick holes in my roof of mineral felt,
Beg to be changed to a multi-channel town.

Tears, temper, screams, my battered frame endures
By dint of carpentry, no miracle cures.

PRISON

Losing your pen in the body-search behind
My dustbin-columned classical façade,
You're led by intercrural routes to find
Your gypsy friend, trussed in my fixed abode.

Before he lost his capricious boyhood, grew
A centaur's beard, hooves, haunches in relief,
Did you cage him with hubristic love? You knew
His touching thievery often gave you life.

Free to face across doubly screened zoo wire,
Stop-watched by warders in a cell, you meet,
Deterred by a faecal smell, beyond desire
Where words fail to regenerate, but cheat.

Poor old people he robbed in bed at night.
What sentence did your teaching help him write?

Lobawn, he calls me in shelta, his duck nest
Under a thorn-bush on a petering out lane;
Wattled with hazel cut from the remotest
Copse of a departed ascendancy demesne.

Fourteen lithe rods, carved into wish-bones, keep
My head up in the rain. My tarred and buttered
Skin he's smoked and cured. Rats from a trash-heap
Steal bits of his begged bread, but he's not bothered.

Thrown back by cheap wine on to his last straw
He finds I can help the pain. His seed has spread
From road to road: boys gathering scrap in new
Pick-ups, girls as young as Juliet wedded.

It dawns on me, when his bantam cock crows,
I'll house him till he dies, wherever he goes.

NEW GRANGE

Brought to a brumal standstill, here I lie
Obliquely floored, mouth curbed by stones that speak
In pick-dressed spirals, egghead sucked bone dry,
Waiting for dawn inside my skull to streak.

Sungod and riverbride died in my bed
To live as bead and elkshorn under earth.
One cairn eye stayed open to feed the dead
A ray of wintry hope, fixed on rebirth.

Up a dark passage, brightening from far back,
A sunbeam seeks my carved leakproof abode.
As pollen dust ignites my pebble stack
The tomb I've made becomes a vivid road.

Once a year it may strike me, a pure gift
Making light work, a mound of greywacke lift.

FRIARY

Each time you breathe my name—Ross Errilly—
Young leaf-growth rustles in the druid wood,
Felled to convert my land so thoroughly
Stone crosses stand on grass where forest stood.

Here the rain harps on ruins, plucking lost
Tunes from my structure, which the wind pours through
In jackdaw desecration, carping at the dust
And leprous sores my towers like beggars show.

Now my fish-ponds hold no water. Doors and aisles
Are stacked with donors' tombs, badly invested,
A gift for peeping toms: my lecherous gargoyles
Hacked off by thieves, the bones unresurrected.

Here, too, buried in rhyme, lovers lie dead,
Engraved in words that live each time they're read.

BEEHIVE CELL

There's no comfort inside me, only a small
Hart's-tongue sprouting square, with pyramidal headroom
For one man alone kneeling down: a smell
Of peregrine mutes and eremitical boredom.

Once, in my thirteen hundred years on this barren
Island, have I felt a woman giving birth,
On her own in my spinal cerebellic souterrain,
To a living child, as she knelt on earth.

She crawled under my lintel that purgatorial night
Her menfolk marooned her out of their coracle
To pick dillisk and sloke. What hand brought a light
With angelica root for the pain of her miracle?

Three days she throve in me, suckling the child,
Doing all she had to do, the sea going wild.

NATURAL SON

Before the spectacled professor snipped
The cord, I heard your birth-cry flood the ward,
And lowered your mother's tortured head, and wept.
The house you'd left would need to be restored.

No worse pain could be borne, to bear the joy
Of seeing you come in a slow dive from the womb,
Pushed from your fluid home, pronounced "a boy".
You'll never find so well equipped a room.

No house we build could hope to satisfy
Every small need, now that you've made this move
To share our loneliness, much as we try
Our vocal skill to wall you round with love.

This day you crave so little, we so much
For you to live, who need our merest touch.

"Woman of the House" (13): **Charles James Lever** (1806–1872), author of *Charles O'Malley* and other novels. "His vivid rollicking pictures of military life and of the hard-drinking fox-hunting Irish society of his days were very popular." *Oxford Companion to English Literature.* Sir Paul Harvey. **Samuel Lover** (1797–1868), Irish novelist and song-writer, author of "Rory O'Moore" and "Handy Andy." **Edith Somerville** (1858–1949) **and Martin Ross** (1862–1915), joint authors of *Some Experiences of an Irish R.M.* (1890) and *The Real Charlotte* (1894).

"The Last Galway Hooker" (19): The title refers to a single-masted fishing boat used off the coast of Ireland. **The Claddagh,** on the western side of Galway city, across the Corrib river, was in 1922 occupied mostly by fishermen and their families, whose small, congested houses were thatched and lacking in modern amenities. The name signifies a flat stony sea-shore. **The Treaty** between Britain and Ireland ended the Irish War for Independence (1919–21) and occasioned the Civil War (1922–23) between the Irish Free State and the Irish Republican Army.

"Rosroe, 1955" (40): (signifying "red peninsular") is a promontory between the Big and the Little Killary harbours on the extreme north-west corner of County Galway, exposed to the Atlantic. A cottage used as a coast guard station on the Rosroe Quay in the time of the great famine (1845–48) was rented by the poet from 1951–1956. After his marriage to Patricia Avis in 1955, the couple lived there during the summer. The philosopher, Ludwig Wittgenstein, had stayed there in 1949, leaving a legend that inspired the poem **"Wittgenstein and the Birds"** (6) in 1953; and in 1982, long after the house had been turned into a youth hostel, **"Killary Hostel"** (189).

"The Battle of Aughrim" (42) [See headnote to the poem]: **"Gouldings Grows"** was the advertising slogan of an Irish fertiliser company in the Sixties.

"The God Who Eats Corn" (74): At the end of the nineteenth century, there was no word in Sindebele to describe the white man who came to settle in central Africa, so he was called "the god who eats corn," meaning that although he had godlike powers, he had to eat, and to die. The poet's father, Sir William Lindsay Murphy, who was born in an Irish rectory, retired from the British Colonial Service as Governor of the Bahamas. He then settled in Southern Rhodesia in 1950 on virgin land, where he and his wife established a farm, and later built a school to educate 250 children of farm workers through seven grades. There were no schools in the area, and the policy of white settlers was to keep Africans ignorant in order to ensure a supply of cheap, submissive, manual labourers. Sir William's paternal grandfather had emerged from ignorance and poverty in Ireland through the Carlow village school (170) of which he became the master in 1840. The poem was written in Ireland in the second half of 1963, when direct colonial rule by Britain ended in central Africa with the emergence of Zambia and Malawi, which Sir William approved. It deploys with irony the diction of the period to voice the mindsets of the period, whether racist, revolutionary, multicultural, or democratic, and to place Sir William on the farm he loved, where he and his wife and sister—she taught in the school unpaid—tried to do some good, in a bad historical and political situation. **"Sundowners"** are drinks at the time of sunset. **"Munt"** is an insulting word for a black African, used in Rhodesia and South Africa. **"B.S.A.,"** The British South Africa police force, established in the time of Cecil Rhodes, still used that name in 1963. "*Indaba*": In tribal society, the chieftain decided his policy after hearing advice from his counsellors in the shade of a large tree. This counsel was called the indaba. The tree could be any kind of large African tree, a mopani, a fig, or, most likely, a msasa, a lovely deciduous tree of the bush.

"Little Hunger" (84) refers to a place near Cleggan, County Galway, called Aughrusbeg, meaning "little hunger," where many people died during the Famine, or subsequently emigrated. The pink granite that was used to build the poet's house, **"New Forge"** (196), was obtained from the ruins of their houses.

Tony White (1930–1976): Anglo-French writer, translator, actor, footballer, craftsman, fisherman, and charismatic friend. In 1957, he tore up a contract to play leading Shakespearean roles with the Old Vic, and after some odd jobs such as lighting old gas lamps in the streets of London's East End, he came to the west of Ireland, where he stayed for long periods at Cleggan and Inishbofin. There the poet met him in 1959, as described in **"Double Negative"** (88), a title suggested by Tony. In 1965, he ghost-wrote *Contempt of Court*, a finely written memoir of the famous ex-convict and jail-breaker Alfred Hinds, who claimed, and finally proved in court, that he had been wrongly convicted of the armed robbery of a store in London. Tony's personality, ideas, criticism, conscience, sense of humour, and craftsmanship profoundly influenced the poet and his poetry. Tony's early death was the result of a football injury on an icy pitch in London during a strike by doctors.

"Ardilaun" (101) is the Irish name meaning "High Island," famous for its seventh century hermitage. Situated two miles off the west coast of Ireland, between Slyne Head and Inishbofin, it contains eighty acres of rock, mostly quartzite and mica schist, with a covering of wild grasses and flowers such as thrift and sea campion. The poet purchased the island in 1969, to preserve as a wild life sanctuary, especially for birds and grey Atlantic seals. In 1971, he renovated one room of the derelict old (1827) **"Miners' Hut"** (194) and wrote much of the High Island poetry, including **"Nocturne"** (102), **"Stormpetrel"** (107), **"Ball's Cove"** (89), and **"Seals at High Island"** (83), between 1969 and 1973, during days and nights he spent there completely alone.

The Mirror Wall (149) is a sequence of sixty-two translations or imitations of graffiti poems—eight of which appear here—inscribed in the shining surface of a remote, fortified rock in the central province of Sri Lanka. The graffiti poems offer a variety of responses to mysterious, erotic "golden" women in frescoes painted on the rock above this "mirror wall." The poet spent five of his childhood years in Ceylon, where his father was the last British Mayor of Colombo, and returned fifty years later to Sri Lanka for five extended visits.

The Price of Stone: (155) *The Price of Stone* contains sonnets relevant to all phases of the poet's life and commensurate with the poet's journals, to be published by Granta Books in the form of a memoir in 2002.

"Folly" (157): At the top of Killiney Hill in south County Dublin, a tall, useless ornamental building was constructed at the behest of a landlord in 1742 to glorify his estate. This gazebo or folly consists of a plastered stone spire superimposed upon an equilateral cube. It bears on a marble plaque the declaration of a vain, Anglo-Irish do-gooder:

Last year being hard with the poor,
the walks about these hills and this
were erected by John Maypass,
    June 1742.

When the poet moved from Cleggan in 1980, to a house in Killiney called "Knockbrack" (164), he formed a habit of running to the top of the hill and back every morning before breakfast. Standing at the folly one can see the whole of Dublin and Dublin Bay from Howth Head to Bray Head, with the Sugarloaf mountain stretching away into the Wicklow hills. On Easter Sunday 1981, the poet began to identify with this decadent, epicene, vandalised Anglo-Irish relic, in a poem giving ironic voice to the folly and the folly's exalted point of view. That led to the writing of nearly all the other sonnets in *The Price of Stone* sequence, in which the persona of each poem is a different structure—house, tent, caravan, school, castle, tenement, ice rink, pub, prison, friary, sauna, passage grave, monument, or beehive cell—reflecting aspects of the poet's life at different times and places."

"Nelson's Pillar" (160): On a commanding site in the centre of Dublin, the Doric column, topped by a statue of Nelson, was erected by subscription of the merchants of Dublin in 1808–09, half a century before the pillar was built in Trafalgar Square, to commemorate the naval victory of Trafalgar. Since the partial independence of Ireland in 1922, political and other efforts were made to have the statue of Nelson either removed or replaced by one of the Blessed Virgin Mary. An offer by the Belfast City Council to transfer it from Dublin and re-erect it in Belfast was turned down. W. B. Yeats, speaking in the Irish Senate in 1923, said: "It represents the feeling of Protestant Ireland for a man who helped to break the power of Napoleon. The life and work of the people who erected it is a part of our tradition. I think we should accept the whole past of this nation and not pick and choose. However it is not a beautiful object."

Shortly before the fiftieth anniversary of the Easter 1916 Rising, a bomb timed to explode at night blew off the top, and a few nights later, on the 14th March 1966, authorised by the government, a controlled explosion demolished the stump that remained. The flash emitted by the explosive was described by an onlooker as red, white, and blue. "People sang and danced as they waited for the count-down, and there was a great deal of cheering and clapping when the pillar fell," according to the *Irish Times*.

"Waterkeeper's Bothy" (190): The hut or cottage of a water bailiff or watchman charged with protecting his employer's fishing rights from poachers. In 1952, the poet had a night job as a watchman on eight miles of the Erriff River in County Mayo.

"Kylemore Castle" (191) was built in 1867 for an English industrialist called Mitchell Henry, who acquired a vast estate of mountain land, lakes, and rivers in Connemara. When his wife died, her body was embalmed and kept in a glass coffin, which used to be wheeled into the dining-room once a year for Christmas dinner, according to local legend. The estate was subsequently acquired by the Duke of Manchester, who entertained King Edward VII there. The castle became an abbey from about 1922 onwards, home to a Benedictine order of nuns whose convent at Ypres had been destroyed by German shelling in the 1914–1918 war. With his sister and brother, the poet attended classes taught by nuns, at the abbey in 1935, when his family were staying at a house nearby (**"Planter Stock"** [174]) with a view of the **"Connemara Quay"** (170) close to the **"Letterfrack Industrial School"** (177).

Later that year, the poet's brother and he began to board at a school called **"Baymount"** (178) in Clontarf, on the north side of Dublin, where the custom was for the youngest boy (the poet at age 8) to be challenged to take a bite out of a burning candle on the Hallow E'en cake. They were moved in 1937 to the **"Choir School"** (180) at **"Canterbury Cathedral"** (179) until war interrupted their musical education in May 1940, when the brothers went home to be taught by tutors at **"Milford: East Wing"** (183) attached to the poet's **"Birth Place"** (171) the big house of his grandfather on the Mayo-Galway border, where **"Suntrap"** (181) and **"Gate Lodge"** (182) are also set.

Having won a scholarship to the King's School, Canterbury in 1941, the poet spent four terms at its wartime location in Cornwall, in the **"Carlyon Bay Hotel"** (184). Then in 1943, he moved to **"Wellington College"** (185) in Berkshire, founded to commemorate the Duke of Wellington, as was the **"Wellington Testimonial"** (161) in Phoenix Park, Dublin. Winning a scholarship to Oxford at age seventeen, he was tutored there by C. S. Lewis, as in **"Oxford Staircase"** (186).

"Hexagon" (195): The word "rupestral" means "growing on rocks." The poet's

Hexagon on Omey Island was built of local granite on top of a granite out-crop, in the summer of 1975.

"New Forge" (196): The word "exuviate," used of lobsters or crayfish, means to cast off an old shell in order to grow a new. The house was built for the poet in 1965 and sold in 1979, when he moved to **"Knockbrack"** (164) in south County Dublin.

"Horse-Drawn Caravan" (198), **"Old Dispensary"** (199), **"Chalet"** (200), and **"Wattle Tent"** (202) draw on the poet's experience of housing two large families of travellers (formerly known as itinerants or tinkers) in the west of Ireland between 1967 and 1975.

"Beehive Cell" (205): At a small hermitage, founded in the seventh century on High Island, off the north-west coast of Connemara, there remains a clo-chan or stone hut, built in the shape of a beehive, that has survived, though in ruins, since its erection. It became an eyrie of hawks; and once, in a time of hunger, it sheltered a poor, pregnant woman who was marooned for three days alone without food. Her husband had left her on the island to pick grass and edible seaweed, such as "dillisk" and "sloke," but a storm prevented him bringing her home. When the sea calmed, and he rowed out to rescue her, she climbed down a cliff and stepped into his curragh carrying her baby. She said an angel had given her a hand, and a garb for the child. The poem was written shortly before the birth of Anya Barnett's and the poet's son in Dublin, on the 29th January 1982. **"Natural Son"** (206) was written two days later.

Collected Poems gathers most of the poems from Richard Murphy's principal volumes: *The Archaeology of Love* (Dolmen 1955); *Sailing to an Island* (Faber & Faber 1963; Chilmark Press 1964); *The Battle of Aughrim* (Faber & Faber / Knopf, 1964); *High Island* (Faber & Faber 1974); *High Island: New and Selected Poems* (Harper & Row 1975); *Selected Poems* (Faber & Faber 1979); *Care* (Cornamona 1982); *The Price of Stone* (Faber & Faber 1985); *The Price of Stone and Earlier Poems* (Wake Forest 1985); *New Selected Poems* (Faber & Faber 1989); *The Mirror Wall* (Bloodaxe / Wolfhound / Wake Forest 1989).

Poems conceived or drafted during the period of the major volumes or otherwise arising from these periods appear in the appropriate sections. We gratefully acknowledge that some of these uncollected poems first appeared in *Agenda, The Irish Times, Irish University Review, The New Yorker, The New York Review of Books, Poetry* (Chicago), *Poetry Ireland Review, The Princeton University Library Chronicle, TLS, The Recorder,* and *The Sunday Times*.